CW01283030

THE ULTIMATE INSTANT VORTEX AIR FRYER UK COOKBOOK

1500 Days of Delicious, Simple and Easy Recipes for Smart Home Cooking |With Premium Full Colour Pictures

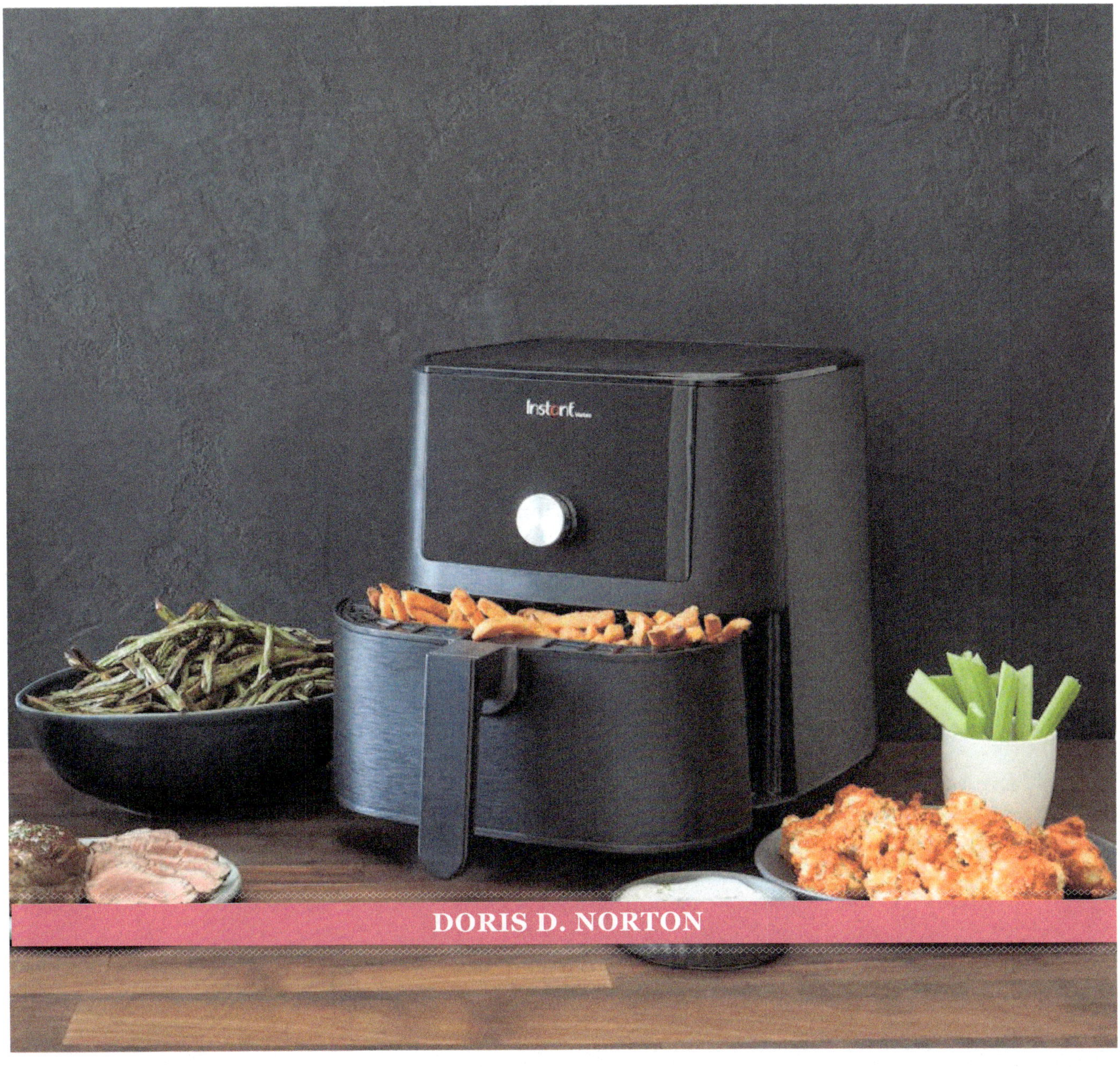

DORIS D. NORTON

Copyright© 2022 By Doris D. Norton Rights Reserved

This book is copyright protected. It is only for personal use. You cannot amend, distribute, sell, use, quote or paraphrase any part of the content within this book, without the consent of the author or publisher.

Under no circumstances will any blame or legal responsibility be held against the publisher, or author, for any damages, reparation, or monetary loss due to the information contained within this book, either directly or indirectly.

Disclaimer Notice:

Please note the information contained within this document is for educational and entertainment purposes only. All effort has been executed to present accurate, up to date, reliable, complete information. No warranties of any kind are declared or implied. Readers acknowledge that the author is not engaged in the rendering of legal, financial, medical or professional advice. The content within this book has been derived from various sources. Please consult a licensed professional before attempting any techniques outlined in this book.

By reading this document, the reader agrees that under no circumstances is the author responsible for any losses, direct or indirect, that are incurred as a result of the use of the information contained within this document, including, but not limited to, errors, omissions, or inaccuracies.

Table of Contents

Introduction	1
Chapter 1	
Breads & Breakfast	2
Potato & Kale Nuggets	3
Bread Rolls	3
Maple Cinnamon Buns	4
Taj Tofu	4
Morning Veggies on Toast	5
Air Fried Vegan Breakfast Bread	5
Paprika Egg Cups	6
Rice Paper Bacon	6
Veg Frittata	7
Italian Breakfast Frittata	7
Breakfast Banana Cookies	8
Air Fryer Broccoli & Tofu Scramble	8
Buttery Eggs	9
Broccoli Casserole	9
Creamy Parmesan Eggs	10
Eggs with Peppers	10
Bacon Cups	10
Chapter 2	
Snacks & Appetizers	11
Potato Chips	12
Brussels Sprouts	12
Garlic Potatoes	13
Chopped Liver with Eggs	13
Baked Tomato & Egg	14
Parmesan Asparagus Fries	14
Turmeric Tempeh	15
Asparagus	15
Spicy Mozzarella Stick	16
Garlic Avocado Balls	16
Zucchini Rolls	17
Pork Rinds	17
Cheese Croquettes with Prosciutto	18
Cilantro Shrimp Balls	18
Cashew Dip	19
Garlic Brussel Sprouts	19
Turmeric Chicken Cubes	20
Broccoli Puree	20
Coriander Fennel	20
Banana Peppers Mix	21
Keto "Potato"	21
Chapter 3	
Chicken and Poultry	22
Chicken Curry	23
Marjoram Chicken	23
Hoisin Glazed Turkey Drumsticks	24
Thai Turkey Wings	24
Air Fryer Moroccan Chicken	25
Easy Blackened Chicken	25
Battered Chicken Thighs	26
Barbecue Drumsticks	26

Turkey Sliders & Chive Mayonnaise	27
Dijon Lime Chicken	27
Cumin Chicken Thighs	28
Cauliflower Stuffed Chicken	28
Pesto Chicken	29
Hoisin Chicken	29
Sun-dried Tomatoes and Chicken Mix	30
Cream Cheese Chicken	30
Ginger Chicken and Lemon Sauce	31
Air-Fried Hot Wings	31
Keto TSO Chicken	32
Jalapeno Chicken Drumsticks	32
Chicken Quesadilla Melt	32
Provolone Chicken Breasts	32

Chapter 4
Beef, Lamb and Pork — 33

Beef & Mushrooms	34
Max's Meatloaf	34
Air-Fried Lamb Chops	35
Roasted Rack of Lamb with Macadamia Crust	35
Onion Carrot Meatloaf	36
Pork Satay with Peanut Sauce	36
Cheese Burgers	37
Meatballs with Sauce	37
Spicy Beef Schnitzel	38
Dijon Pork Chops	38
Pumpkin & Pork Empanadas	39
Coconut Pork and Green Beans	39
Italian Pork	40
Chili Tomato Pork	40
Greek Pork and Spinach	41
Pork and Asparagus	41
Pork Stuffing	42
African Style Pork Shoulder	42
Scallions Pork Chops	42

Chapter 5
Fish and Seafood — 43

Cod Fish Teriyaki with Oysters, Mushrooms & Veggies	44
Crab Buns	44
Salmon with Dill Sauce	45
Grilled Salmon with Capers & Dill	45
Stevia Cod	46
Butter Crab Muffins	46
Tilapia and Kale	47
Air-Fried Asian Style Fish	47
Chili Haddock	48
Rosemary Shrimp Skewers	48
Black Cod with Grapes, Pecans, Fennel & Kale	49
Sweet Tilapia Fillets	49
Chili and Oregano Tilapia	49

Chapter 6
Vegetarian Recipes — 50

Cumin, Chili & Squash	51
Pineapple Sticks with Yogurt Dip	51
Low-Carb Zucchini Roll-Ups	52
Coconut Broccoli	52
Broccoli and Cranberries Mix	53
Zucchini Fries & Roasted Garlic Aioli	53
Coconut Kohlrabi Mash	54
Roasted Kabocha Squash	54
Broccoli and Scallions Sauce	55
Zucchini and Squash Mix	55
Zucchini, Carrots & Yellow Squash	56
Cauliflower Casserole	56
Vinegar Cauliflower Mix	56

Chapter 7
Desserts and Staples — 57

Banana Oatmeal Cookies	58
Sweet & Crisp Bananas	58
Coconut Prune Cookies	58
Delicious Clafoutis	58
Pear & Apple Crisp with Walnuts	58
Lemon Pie	59
Shortbread Fingers	59
Cream Cheese Scones	59
Almond Orange Cake	59
Sugar Butter Fritters	60
Air-Fried Apricots in Whiskey Sauce	60
Date & Hazelnut Cookies	60
Berry Pie	60
Butter Donuts	60

Appendix 1 Measurement Conversion Chart — 61
Appendix 2 The Dirty Dozen and Clean Fifteen — 62
Appendix 3 Index — 63

Introduction

First of all, thank you for reading my book right now, whether it's a gift or you purchased it, I am grateful to you for taking the time to read it. This means a lot.

This is not my first time writing a book but this book is very special and personal for me. It's because I wrote this book with a deep sense of responsibility and love.

I started cooking at a very young age and eventually cooking became more than just a hobby and turned into my passion. I loved cooking, and I especially loved cooking for my loved ones. My little family consists of my mom, dad, and my brother. So most of the time when I cooked for my family I made tasty, delicious, and to tell the truth unhealthy, oily foods that had less nutritional value. That food made them happy but I didn't ever pay attention to the fact that those foods were unhealthy and ultimately bad for them.

Reality hit me when my dad suddenly had a cardiac arrest a few years ago and the doctor said that he had developed heart blockage due to eating excessive oily and junk food. Frankly speaking, I was the one to blame, I was the ignorant one who didn't pay attention to the nutritional value of foods and my ignorance eventually resulted in something so fatal. The fact is, I could've lost my dad forever but we were very fortunate that he was given a second chance.

After this incident, the doctor prescribed him fewer medicines and medical treatments and advised him to change his diet and move towards eating healthier food. He started to change his diet after consulting a dietician but he was unhappy. Due to eating all those boring and rather blunt food, eventually he just hated to eat.

2020 had been a tough year for everyone worldwide and it was the same for my family. That year a friend of mine gifted me an Instant Vortx Airfryer. At first, I wasn't certain what to do with it. Then I started looking for air fryer recipes, and there were thousands of recipes online so I started trying them out. Soon afterward, I started trying out my recipes, most of them were successful, but some of them failed obviously. But the best thing that happened is that my dad started to love eating food again, foods that were not only healthy but also tasty.

This became my biggest inspiration for me. And I fell in love with air frying and for a good reason. Besides, my dad was not only healthy but happy again and that's what happened the most to me.

This method of cooking changed my life, literally and metaphorically and I will be forever grateful for that. I hope this book of mine would help you in some way too, lots of love and best wishes to you. And Merry Christmas!

Chapter 1
Breads & Breakfast

Potato & Kale Nuggets

Prep Time: 5 minutes | Cook Time: 20 minutes | Serves 4

- 1 tsp. extra virgin olive oil
- 1 clove of garlic, minced
- 4 cups kale, rinsed and chopped
- 2 cups potatoes, boiled and mashed
- 1/8 cup milk
- Salt and pepper to taste
- Vegetable oil

1. Preheat your Air Fryer at 390°F.
2. In a skillet over medium heat, fry the garlic in the olive oil, until it turns golden brown. Cook with the kale for an additional 3 minutes and remove from the heat.
3. Mix the mashed potatoes, kale and garlic in a bowl. Throw in the milk and sprinkle with some salt and pepper as desired.
4. Shape the mixture into nuggets and spritz each one with a little vegetable oil. Put in the basket of your fryer and leave to cook for 15 minutes, shaking the basket halfway through cooking to make sure the nuggets fry evenly.

Bread Rolls

Prep Time: 10 minutes | Cook Time: 20 minutes | Serves 5

- 5 large potatoes, boiled and mashed
- Salt and pepper to taste
- 1 tbsp. olive oil
- ½ tsp. mustard seeds
- 2 small onions, chopped
- ½ tsp. turmeric
- 2 sprigs curry leaves
- 8 slices of bread, brown sides discarded
- 2 green chilis, seeded and chopped
- 1 bunch coriander, chopped

1. Preheat your Air Fryer at 400°F.
2. Put the mashed potatoes in a bowl and sprinkle on salt and pepper. Set to one side.
3. Fry the mustard seeds in a little olive oil over a medium-low heat, stirring continuously, until they sputter.
4. Add in the onions and cook until they turn translucent. Add the curry leaves and turmeric powder and stir. Cook for a further 2 minutes until fragrant.
5. Remove the pan from the heat and combine the contents with the potatoes. Remove from heat and add to the potatoes. Mix in the green chilies and coriander.
6. Wet the bread slightly and drain of any excess liquid.
7. Spoon a small amount of the potato mixture into the center of the bread and enclose the bread around the filling, sealing it entirely. Continue until the rest of the bread and filling is used up. Brush each bread roll with some oil and transfer to the basket of your fryer.
8. Cook for 15 minutes, gently shaking the fryer basket at the halfway point to ensure each roll is cooked evenly.

Maple Cinnamon Buns

Prep Time: 1 hour | Cook Time: 55 minutes | Serves 9

- 3/4 cup unsweetened milk
- 4 tbsp. maple syrup
- 1 ½ tbsp. active yeast
- 1 tbsp. ground flaxseed
- 1 tbsp. coconut oil, melted
- 1 cup flour
- 1 ½ cup flour
- 2 tsp. cinnamon powder
- ½ cup pecan nuts, toasted
- 2 ripe bananas, sliced
- 4 Medjool dates, pitted
- ¼ cup sugar

1. Over a low heat, warm the milk until it is tepid. Combine with the yeast and maple syrup, waiting 5 – 10 minutes to allow the yeast to activate.
2. In the meantime, put 3 tbsp. of water and the flaxseed in a bowl and stir together. This is your egg substitute. Let the flaxseed absorb the water for about 2 minutes.
3. Pour the coconut oil into the bowl, then combine the flaxseed mixture with the yeast mixture.
4. In a separate bowl, mix together one tbsp. of the cinnamon powder and the white and flour. Add the yeast-flaxseed mixture and mix to create a dough.
5. Dust a flat surface with flour. On this surface, knead the dough with your hands for a minimum of 10 minutes.
6. Grease a large bowl and transfer the dough inside. Cover with a kitchen towel or saran wrap. Let sit in a warm, dark place for an hour so that the dough may rise.
7. In the meantime, prepare the filling. Mix the banana slices, dates, and pecans together before throwing in a tbsp. of cinnamon powder.
8. Set the Air Fryer to 390°F and allow to warm. On your floured surface, flatten the dough with a rolling pin, making it thin. Spoon the pecan mixture onto the dough and spread out evenly.
9. Roll up the dough and then slice it in nine. Transfer the slices to a dish small enough to fit in the fryer, set the dish inside, and cook for 30 minutes.
10. Top with a thin layer of sugar before serving.

Taj Tofu

Prep Time: 10 minutes | Cook Time: 30 minutes | Serves 4

- 1 block firm tofu, pressed and cut into 1-inch thick cubes
- 2 tbsp. soy sauce
- 2 tsp. sesame seeds, toasted
- 1 tsp. rice vinegar
- 1 tbsp. cornstarch

1. Set your Air Fryer at 400°F to warm.
2. Add the tofu, soy sauce, sesame seeds and rice vinegar in a bowl together and mix well to coat the tofu cubes. Then cover the tofu in cornstarch and put it in the basket of your fryer.
3. Cook for 25 minutes, giving the basket a shake at five-minute intervals to ensure the tofu cooks evenly.

Morning Veggies on Toast

Prep Time: 2 minutes | Cook Time: 11 minutes | Serves 4

- 1 tablespoon olive oil
- ½ cup soft goat cheese
- 2 tablespoons softened butter
- 4 slices French bread
- 2 green onions, sliced
- 1 small yellow squash, sliced
- 1 cup button mushrooms, sliced
- 1 red bell pepper, cut into strips

1. Sprinkle your air fryer with olive oil and preheat it to 350°Fahrenheit. Mix the red bell peppers, squash, mushrooms and green onions, cook them for 7-minutes. Place vegetables on a plate and set aside.
2. Spread the bread slices with butter and place into air fryer, with butter side up. Toast for 4-minutes.
3. Spread the goat cheese on toasted bread and top with veggies. Serve warm.

Air Fried Vegan Breakfast Bread

Prep Time: 5 minutes | Cook Time: 10 minutes | Serves 2

- 1 vegan bread loaf, large
- 2 teaspoons chives
- 2 tablespoons nutritional yeast
- 2 tablespoons garlic puree
- 2 tablespoons olive oil
- Salt and pepper to taste

1. Preheat your air fryer to 375°Fahrenheit. Slice the bread loaf (not all the way through). In a bowl, combine the garlic puree, olive oil, and nutritional yeast.
2. Add this mixture on top of the bread loaf. Sprinkle loaf with chives and season with salt and pepper.
3. Place loaf inside of your air fryer and cook for 10-minutes.

Paprika Egg Cups
Prep Time: 10 minutes | Cook Time: 3 minutes | Serves 2

- 2 eggs
- 1 tablespoon cream cheese
- 1 teaspoon smoked paprika

1. Crack the eggs into the ramekins and top them with smoked paprika and cream cheese.
2. Cook the eggs in the air fryer at 400F for 3 minutes.

Rice Paper Bacon
Prep Time: 5 minutes | Cook Time: 30 minutes | Serves 4

- 4 pieces white rice paper,
- cut into 1-inch thick strips
- 2 tablespoons water
- 2 tablespoons liquid smoke
- 2 tablespoons cashew butter
- 3 tablespoons soy sauce or tamari

1. Preheat your air fryer to 350°Fahrenheit. In a mixing bowl, add soy sauce, cashew butter, liquid smoke, and water, mix well. Soak the rice paper in this mixture for 5 minutes.
2. Place the rice paper in air fryer and do not overlap pieces. Air fry for 15-minutes or until crispy. Serve with steamed vegetables!

Veg Frittata

Prep Time: 5 minutes | Cook Time: 30 minutes | Serves 2

- ¼ cup milk
- 1 zucchini
- ½ bunch asparagus
- ½ cup mushrooms
- ½ cup spinach or baby spinach
- ½ cup red onion, sliced
- 4 eggs
- ½ tbsp. olive oil
- 5 tbsp. feta cheese, crumbled
- 4 tbsp. cheddar, grated
- ¼ bunch chives, minced
- Sea salt and pepper to taste

1. In a bowl, mix together the eggs, milk, salt and pepper.
2. Cut up the zucchini, asparagus, mushrooms and red onion into slices. Shred the spinach using your hands.
3. Over a medium heat, stir-fry the vegetables for 5 – 7 minutes with the olive oil in a non-stick pan.
4. Place some parchment paper in the base of a baking tin. Pour in the vegetables, followed by the egg mixture. Top with the feta and grated cheddar.
5. Set the Air Fryer at 320°F and allow to warm for five minutes.
6. Transfer the baking tin to the fryer and allow to cook for 15 minutes. Take care when removing the frittata from the Air Fryer and leave to cool for 5 minutes.
7. Top with the minced chives and serve.

Italian Breakfast Frittata

Prep Time: 5 minutes | Cook Time: 10 minutes | Serves 2

- 4 cherry tomatoes, sliced into halves
- ½ Italian sausage, sliced
- ½ teaspoon Italian seasoning
- 3 eggs
- 2-ounces parmesan cheese, shredded
- 1 tablespoon parsley, chopped
- Salt and pepper to taste

1. Preheat your air fryer to 360°Fahrenheit. Put the sausage and cherry tomatoes into baking dish and cook for 5-minutes.
2. Crack eggs into small bowl, add parsley, Italian seasoning and mix well by whisking. Pour egg mixture over sausage and cherry tomatoes and place back into air fryer to cook for an additional 5-minutes. Serve warm.

Breakfast Banana Cookies
Prep Time: 5 minutes | Cook Time: 20 minutes | Serves 6

- 3 ripe bananas
- 1 teaspoon vanilla extract
- 1/3 cup olive oil
- 1 cup dates, pitted and chopped
- 2 cups rolled oats

1. Preheat your air fryer to 350°Fahrenheit. In a bowl, mash bananas and add the rest of the ingredients and mix well. Allow ingredients to rest in the fridge for 10-minutes.
2. Cut some parchment paper to fit inside of your air fryer basket. Drop teaspoonful of mixture on parchment paper, making sure not to overlap the cookies. Cook the cookies for 20-minutes and serve with some almond milk.

Air Fryer Broccoli & Tofu Scramble
Prep Time: 5 minutes | Cook Time: 30 minutes | Serves 3

- 4 cups broccoli florets
- 1 block tofu, chopped finely
- 2 ½ cups red potatoes, chopped
- 2 tablespoons olive oil
- 2 tablespoons tamari
- 1 teaspoon turmeric powder
- ½ teaspoon garlic powder
- ½ teaspoon onion powder
- ½ cup onion, chopped

1. Preheat your air fryer to 400°Fahrenheit. Mix the potatoes in a bowl with half of the olive oil. Place the potatoes into a baking dish that will fit into your air fryer and cook them for 15-minutes.
2. Combine the remaining olive oil, tofu, tamari, turmeric, garlic powder and onion powder. Stir in the chopped onions. Add the broccoli florets. Pour this mixture on top of the air-fried potatoes and cook for an additional 15-minutes. Serve warm.

Buttery Eggs
Prep Time: 5 minutes | Cook Time: 20 minutes | Serves 4

- 2 tablespoons butter, melted
- 6 teaspoons basil pesto
- 1 cup mozzarella cheese, grated
- 6 eggs, whisked
- 2 tablespoons basil, chopped
- A pinch of salt and black pepper

1. In a bowl, mix all the ingredients except the butter and whisk them well.
2. Preheat your Air Fryer at 360 degrees F, drizzle the butter on the bottom, spread the eggs mix, cook for 20 minutes and serve for breakfast.

Broccoli Casserole
Prep Time: 5 minutes | Cook Time: 25 minutes | Serves 4

- 1 broccoli head, florets separated and roughly chopped
- 2 ounces cheddar cheese, grated
- 4 eggs, whisked
- 1 cup almond milk
- 2 teaspoons cilantro, chopped
- Salt and black pepper to the taste

1. In a bowl, mix the eggs with the milk, cilantro, salt and pepper and whisk.
2. Put the broccoli in your air fryer, add the eggs mix over it, spread, sprinkle the cheese on top, cook at 350 degrees F for 25 minutes, divide between plates and serve for breakfast.

Creamy Parmesan Eggs
Prep Time: 10 minutes | Cook Time: 8 minutes | Serves 4

- 4 eggs
- 1 tablespoon heavy cream
- 1 oz Parmesan, grated
- 1 teaspoon dried parsley
- 3 oz kielbasa, chopped
- 1 teaspoon coconut oil

1. Toss the coconut oil in the air fryer basket and melt it at 385F. It will take about 2-3 minutes. Meanwhile, crack the eggs in the mixing bowl. Add heavy cream and dried parsley. Whisk the mixture. Put the chopped kielbasa in the melted coconut oil and cook it for 4 minutes at 385F.
2. After this, add the whisked egg mixture, Parmesan, and stir with the help of the fork. Cook the eggs for 2 minutes. Then scramble them well and cook for 2 minutes more or until they get the desired texture.

Eggs with Peppers
Prep Time: 5 minutes | Cook Time: 20 minutes | Serves 4

- 2 bell peppers, sliced
- 4 eggs, beaten
- 1 teaspoon avocado oil
- ½ teaspoon white pepper

1. Brush the air fryer basket with avocado oil.
2. Then mix the bell peppers with white pepper and put inside the air fryer basket.
3. Pour the beaten eggs over the bell peppers and bake the meal at 360F for 20 minutes.

Bacon Cups
Prep Time: 10 minutes | Cook Time: 10 minutes | Serves 3

- 3 eggs
- ½ teaspoon ground paprika
- 3 bacon slices
- 1 teaspoon avocado oil
- 1 teaspoon chives, chopped

1. Brush the ramekins with avocado oil.
2. Arrange the bacon slices in every ramekin in the shape of the circle and bake at 370F for 7 minutes.
3. After this, crack the eggs in the center of every ramekin and bake the meal at 365F for 3 minutes more.
4. Sprinkle the cooked eggs with chives and ground paprika.

Chapter 2
Snacks & Appetizers

Potato Chips

Prep Time: 30 minutes | Cook Time: 40 minutes | Serves 4

- 2 large potatoes, peel and sliced
- 1 tbsp. rosemary
- 3.5 oz. sour cream
- ¼ tsp. salt

1. Place the potato slices in water and allow to absorb for 30 minutes.
2. Drain the potato slices and transfer to a large bowl. Toss with the rosemary, sour cream, and salt.
3. Pre-heat the Air Fryer to 320°F
4. Put the coated potato slices in the fryer's basket and cook for 35 minutes. Serve hot

Brussels Sprouts

Prep Time: 5 minutes | Cook Time: 10 minutes | Serves 2

- 2 cups Brussels sprouts, sliced in half
- 1 tbsp. balsamic vinegar
- 1 tbsp. olive oil
- ¼ tsp. salt

1. Toss all of the ingredients together in a bowl, coating the Brussels sprouts well.
2. Place the sprouts in the Air Fryer basket and air fry at 400°F for 10 minutes, shaking the basket at the halfway point.

Garlic Potatoes
Prep Time: 10 minutes | Cook Time: 30 minutes | Serves 4

- 1 lb. russet baking potatoes
- 1 tbsp. garlic powder
- 1 tbsp. freshly chopped parsley
- ½ tsp. salt
- ¼ tsp. black pepper
- 1 – 2 tbsp. olive oil

1. Wash the potatoes and pat them dry with clean paper towels.
2. Pierce each potato several times with a fork.
3. Place the potatoes in a large bowl and season with the garlic powder, salt and pepper.
4. Pour over the olive oil and mix well.
5. Pre-heat the Air Fryer to 360°F.
6. Place the potatoes in the fryer and cook for about 30 minutes, shaking the basket a few times throughout the cooking time.
7. Garnish the potatoes with the chopped parsley and serve with butter, sour cream or another dipping sauce if desired.

Chopped Liver with Eggs
Prep Time: 5 minutes | Cook Time: 12 minutes | Serves 2

- 2 large eggs
- 1 lb. sliced liver
- Salt and pepper to taste
- 1 tablespoon cream
- ½ tablespoon black truffle oil
- 1 tablespoon butter

1. Preheat your air fryer to 340°Fahrenheit. Cut liver into thin slices and place in the fridge. Separate the whites from the yolks of the eggs and put each yolk in a cup.
2. In another bowl, add the cream, the black truffle oil, salt, pepper and beat to combine. Take the liver and arrange half of the mixture in a small ramekin. Pour the white of the egg and divide equally between two ramekins. Put the yolks on top. Surround the yolks with the liver and cook for 12-minutes. Serve cool.

Baked Tomato & Egg
Prep Time: 5 minutes | Cook Time: 20 minutes | Serves 2

- 2 tomatoes
- 4 eggs
- 1 cup mozzarella cheese, shredded
- Salt and pepper to taste
- 1 tablespoon olive oil
- A few basil leaves

1. Preheat your air fryer to 360°Fahrenheit. Cut each tomato into two halves and place them in a bowl. Season with salt and pepper.
2. Place cheese around the bottom of the tomatoes and add the basil leaves. Break one egg into each tomato slice. Garnish with cheese and drizzle with olive oil. Set the temperature to 360°Fahrenheit and bake for 20-minutes.

Parmesan Asparagus Fries
Prep Time: 3 minutes | Cook Time: 10 minutes | Serves 5

- 1 lb. asparagus spears
- ¼ cup almond flour
- Salt and pepper to taste
- 2 eggs, beaten
- ½ cup Parmesan cheese, grated
- 1 cup pork rinds

1. Preheat your air fryer to 380°Fahrenheit.
2. Combine pork rinds and parmesan cheese in a small bowl. Season with salt and pepper. Line baking sheet with parchment paper.
3. First, dip half the asparagus spears into flour, then into eggs, and finally into pork rind mixture. Place asparagus spears on the baking sheet and bake for 10-minutes.
4. Repeat with remaining spears.

Turmeric Tempeh
Prep Time: 8 minutes | Cook Time: 12 minutes | Serves 4

- 1 teaspoon apple cider vinegar
- 1 tablespoon avocado oil
- ¼ teaspoon ground turmeric
- 6 oz tempeh, chopped

1. Mix avocado oil with apple cider vinegar and ground turmeric.
2. Then sprinkle the tempeh with turmeric mixture and put it in the air fryer basket.
3. Cook the tempeh at 350F for 12 minutes. Shake it after 6 minutes of cooking.

Asparagus
Prep Time: 5 minutes | Cook Time: 10 minutes | Serves 4

- 10 asparagus spears, woody end cut off
- 1 clove garlic, minced
- 4 tbsp. olive oil
- Pepper to taste
- Salt to taste

1. Set the Air Fryer to 400°F and allow to heat for 5 minutes.
2. In a bowl, combine the garlic and oil.
3. Cover the asparagus with this mixture and put it in the fryer basket. Sprinkle over some pepper and salt.
4. Cook for 10 minutes and serve hot.

Spicy Mozzarella Stick
Prep Time: 3 minutes | Cook Time: 5 minutes | Serves 3

- 8-ounces mozzarella cheese, cut into strips
- 2 tablespoons olive oil
- ½ teaspoon salt
- 1 cup pork rinds
- 1 egg
- 1 teaspoon garlic powder
- 1 teaspoon paprika

1. Cut the mozzarella into 6 strips. Whisk the egg along with salt, paprika, and garlic powder. Dip the mozzarella strips into egg mixture first, then into pork rinds. Arrange them on a baking platter and place in the fridge for 30-minutes.
2. Preheat your air fryer to 360°Fahrenheit. Drizzle olive oil into the air fryer. Arrange the mozzarella sticks in the air fryer and cook for about 5-minutes. Make sure to turn them at least twice, to ensure they will become golden on all sides.

Garlic Avocado Balls
Prep Time: 5 minutes | Cook Time: 5 minutes | Serves 4

- 1 avocado, peeled, pitted and mashed
- ¼ cup ghee, melted
- 2 garlic cloves, minced
- 2 spring onions, minced
- 1 chili pepper, chopped
- 1 tablespoon lime juice
- 2 tablespoons cilantro
- A pinch of salt and black pepper
- 4 bacon slices, cooked and crumbled
- Cooking spray

1. In a bowl, mix all the ingredients except the cooking spray, stir well and shape medium balls out of this mix.
2. Place them in your air fryer's basket, grease with cooking spray and cook at 370 degrees F for 5 minutes. Serve as a snack.

Zucchini Rolls

Prep Time: 7 minutes | **Cook Time:** 8 minutes | **Serves 2-4**

- 3 zucchinis, sliced thinly lengthwise with a mandolin or very sharp knife
- 1 tbsp. olive oil
- 1 cup goat cheese
- ¼ tsp. black pepper

1. Preheat your Air Fryer to 390°F.
2. Coat each zucchini strip with a light brushing of olive oil.
3. Combine the sea salt, black pepper and goat cheese.
4. Scoop a small, equal amount of the goat cheese onto the center of each strip of zucchini. Roll up the strips and secure with a toothpick.
5. Transfer to the Air Fryer and cook for 5 minutes until the cheese is warm and the zucchini slightly crispy. If desired, add some tomato sauce on top.

Pork Rinds

Prep Time: 10 minutes | **Cook Time:** 10 minutes | **Serves 3**

- 6 oz pork skin
- 1 tablespoon keto tomato sauce
- 1 teaspoon olive oil

1. Chop the pork skin into the rinds and sprinkle with the sauce and olive oil. Mix up well.
2. Then preheat the air fryer to 400F. Place the pork skin rinds in the air fryer basket in one layer and cook for 10 minutes. Flip the rinds on another side after 5 minutes of cooking.

Cheese Croquettes with Prosciutto
Prep Time: 2 minutes | Cook Time: 7 minutes | Serves 6

- 1 lb. cheddar cheese
- 12 slices of prosciutto
- 1 cup pork rinds
- 4 tablespoons olive oil
- 2 eggs, beaten
- 1 cup almond flour

1. Cut your cheese into 6 equal pieces. Wrap each piece of cheese with 2 prosciutto slices. Place them in the freezer for 5-minutes.
2. Preheat your air fryer to 380°Fahrenheit. Dip the croquettes into the flour first, then the egg, and finally coat them with pork rinds. Place them in air fryer basket and drizzle them with olive oil and cook for 7-minutes.

Cilantro Shrimp Balls
Prep Time: 5 minutes | Cook Time: 15 minutes | Serves 4

- 1 pound shrimp, peeled, deveined and minced
- 1 egg, whisked
- 3 tablespoons coconut, shredded
- ½ cup coconut flour
- 1 tablespoon avocado oil
- 1 tablespoon cilantro, chopped

1. In a bowl, mix all the ingredients, stir well and shape medium balls out of this mix Place the balls in your lined air fryer's basket, cook at 350 degrees F for 15 minutes and serve as an appetizer.

Cashew Dip
Prep Time: 5 minutes | Cook Time: 8 minutes | Serves 6

- ½ cup cashews, soaked in water for 4 hours and drained
- 3 tablespoons cilantro, chopped
- 2 garlic cloves, minced
- 1 teaspoon lime juice
- A pinch of salt and black pepper
- 2 tablespoons coconut milk

1. In a blender, combine all the ingredients, pulse well and transfer to a ramekin. Put the ramekin in your air fryer's basket and cook at 350 degrees F for 8 minutes. Serve as a party dip.

Garlic Brussel Sprouts
Prep Time: 10 minutes | Cook Time: 13 minutes | Serves 6

- 1-pound Brussel sprouts
- 1 teaspoon garlic powder
- 1 teaspoon ground coriander
- 1 tablespoon coconut oil
- 1 tablespoon apple cider vinegar

1. Put coconut oil in the air fryer.
2. Then add Brussel sprouts, garlic powder, ground coriander, and apple cider vinegar.
3. Shake the vegetables gently and cook at 390F for 13 minutes. Shake the Brussel sprouts from time to time to avoid burning.

Turmeric Chicken Cubes
Prep Time: 10 minutes | Cook Time: 12 minutes | Serves 6

- 8 oz chicken fillet
- ½ teaspoon ground black pepper
- ½ teaspoon ground turmeric
- ¼ teaspoon ground coriander
- ½ teaspoon ground paprika
- 3 egg whites, whisked
- 4 tablespoons almond flour
- Cooking spray

1. In the shallow bowl mix up ground black pepper, turmeric, coriander, and paprika. Then chop the chicken fillet on the small cubes and sprinkle them with spice mixture. Stir well and ad egg white. Mix up the chicken and egg whites well.
2. Coat every chicken cube in the almond flour. Preheat the air fryer to 375F. Put the chicken cubes in the air fryer basket in one layer and gently spray with cooking spray. Cook the chicken popcorn for 7 minutes. Then shake the chicken popcorn well and cook it for 5 minutes more.

Broccoli Puree
Prep Time: 10 minutes | Cook Time: 20 minutes | Serves 4

- 1-pound broccoli, chopped
- 1 tablespoon coconut oil
- ¼ cup heavy cream
- 1 teaspoon salt

1. Put coconut oil in the air fryer.
2. Add broccoli, heavy cream, and salt.
3. Cook the mixture for 20 minutes at 365F.
4. Then mash the cooked broccoli mixture until you get the soft puree.

Coriander Fennel
Prep Time: 5 minutes | Cook Time: 15 minutes | Serves 4

- 1 pound fennel bulb, cut into small wedges
- 1 teaspoon ground coriander
- 1 tablespoon avocado oil
- ½ teaspoon salt

1. Rub the fennel bulb with ground coriander, avocado oil, and salt.
2. Put it in the air fryer basket and cook at 390F for 15 minutes. Flip the fennel on another side after 7 minutes of cooking.

Banana Peppers Mix
Prep Time: 10 minutes | Cook Time: 20 minutes | Serves 4

- 8 oz banana peppers, chopped
- 1 tablespoon avocado oil
- 1 tablespoon dried oregano
- 2 tablespoons mascarpone
- 1 cup Monterey Jack cheese, shredded

1. Brush the baking pan with avocado oil.
2. After this, mix banana peppers with dried oregano and mascarpone and put in the prepared baking pan.
3. Top the peppers with Monterey Jack cheese and place in the air fryer basket.
4. Cook the meal at 365F for 20 minutes.

Keto "Potato"
Prep Time: 10 minutes | Cook Time: 20 minutes | Serves 2

- 2 cups cauliflower, chopped
- 1 oz Parmesan, grated
- 1 tablespoon avocado oil

1. Sprinkle the cauliflower with avocado oil and put it in the air fryer.
2. Cook it at 390F for 10 minutes.
3. Then shake the cauliflower and sprinkle with Parmesan.
4. Cook the meal at 390F for 10 minutes more.

Chapter 3
Chicken and Poultry

Chicken Curry
Prep Time: 20 minutes | Cook Time: 40 minutes | Serves 2

- 2 chicken thighs
- 1 small zucchini
- 2 cloves garlic
- 6 dried apricots
- 3 ½ oz. long turnip
- 6 basil leaves
- 1 tbsp. whole pistachios
- 1 tbsp. raisin soup
- 1 tbsp. olive oil
- 1 large pinch salt
- Pinch of pepper
- 1 tsp. curry powder

1. Preheat Air Fryer at 320°F.
2. Cut the chicken into 2 thin slices and chop up the vegetables into bite-sized pieces.
3. In a dish, combine all of the ingredients, incorporating everything well.
4. Place in the fryer and cook for a minimum of 30 minutes.
5. Serve with rice if desired.

Marjoram Chicken
Prep Time: 15 minutes | Cook Time: 45 minutes | Serves 2

- 2 skinless, boneless small chicken breasts
- 2 tbsp. butter
- 1 tsp. sea salt
- ½ tsp. red pepper flakes, crushed
- 2 tsp. marjoram
- ¼ tsp. lemon pepper

1. In a bowl, coat the chicken breasts with all of the other ingredients. Set aside to marinate for 30-60 minutes.
2. Preheat your Air Fryer to 390 degrees.
3. Cook for 20 minutes, turning halfway through cooking time.
4. Check for doneness using an instant-read thermometer. Serve over jasmine rice.

Hoisin Glazed Turkey Drumsticks

Prep Time: 10 minutes plus marinating time | Cook Time: 40 minutes | Serves 4

- 2 turkey drumsticks
- 2 tbsp. balsamic vinegar
- 2 tbsp. dry white wine
- 1 tbsp. extra-virgin olive oil
- 1 sprig rosemary, chopped
- Salt and ground black pepper, to taste
- 2 ½ tbsp. butter, melted
- 2 tbsp. hoisin sauce
- 1 tbsp. honey
- 1 tbsp. honey mustard

1. In a bowl, coat the turkey drumsticks with the vinegar, wine, olive oil, and rosemary. Allow to marinate for 3 hours.
2. Preheat the Air Fryer to 350°F.
3. Sprinkle the turkey drumsticks with salt and black pepper. Cover the surface of each drumstick with the butter.
4. Place the turkey in the fryer and cook at 350°F for 30 - 35 minutes, flipping it occasionally through the cooking time. You may have to do this in batches.
5. In the meantime, make the Hoisin glaze by combining all the glaze ingredients.
6. Pour the glaze over the turkey, and roast for another 5 minutes.
7. Allow the drumsticks to rest for about 10 minutes before carving.

Thai Turkey Wings

Prep Time: 10 minutes | Cook Time: 30 minutes | Serves 4

- ¾ lb. turkey wings, cut into pieces
- 1 tsp. ginger powder
- 1 tsp. garlic powder
- ¾ tsp. paprika
- 2 tbsp. soy sauce
- 1 handful minced lemongrass
- Sea salt flakes and ground black pepper to taste
- 2 tbsp. rice wine vinegar
- ¼ cup peanut butter
- 1 tbsp. sesame oil
- ½ cup Thai sweet chili sauce

1. Boil the turkey wings in a saucepan full of water for 20 minutes.
2. Put the turkey wings in a large bowl and cover them with the remaining ingredients, minus the Thai sweet chili sauce.
3. Transfer to the Air Fryer and fry for 20 minutes at 350°F, turning once halfway through the cooking time. Ensure they are cooked through before serving with the Thai sweet chili sauce, as well as some lemon wedges if desired.

Air Fryer Moroccan Chicken
Prep Time: 5 minutes | Cook Time: 20 minutes | Serves 2

- ½ lb. shredded chicken
- 1 cup chicken broth
- 1 head broccoli, chopped
- 1 carrot, sliced
- Pinch of cinnamon
- Pinch of sea salt
- Pinch of cumin
- Pinch of red pepper

1. In a bowl, mix shredded chicken with cumin, sea salt, red pepper, and cinnamon. Add carrot and broccoli to chicken mixture. Pour in broth and mix well. Let stand for 30-minutes.
2. Add mixture to air fryer and cook for 20-minutes. Serve hot.

Easy Blackened Chicken
Prep Time: 5 minutes | Cook Time: 11 minutes | Serves 2

- 2 medium-sized chicken breasts, skinless and boneless
- 1 tablespoon olive oil
- 3 tablespoons Cajun seasoning
- ½ teaspoon salt

1. Rub the chicken breasts with Cajun seasoning, salt, and sprinkle with olive oil.
2. Preheat your air fryer to 370°Fahrenheit and cook chicken breasts for 7-minutes. Turn over and cook for an additional 4-minutes. Slice and serve.

Battered Chicken Thighs

Prep Time: 5 minutes | Cook Time: 18 minutes | Serves 4

- 1 ½ lbs. chicken thighs
- 2 cups buttermilk
- 1 tablespoon baking powder
- 2 teaspoons black pepper
- 2 cups almond flour
- 2 teaspoons sea salt
- 1 teaspoon cayenne pepper
- 1 tablespoon paprika
- 1 tablespoon garlic powder

1. Place chicken thighs into a bowl. In another bowl, mix buttermilk, salt, pepper, cayenne and black pepper. Pour mixture over chicken thighs. Use foil to cover the bowl, then place in the fridge for 4-hours.
2. Preheat your air fryer to 400°Fahrenheit. Mix flour, baking powder, paprika and garlic powder I a shallow bowl. Line baking dish with parchment paper. Dip chicken thighs in flour mixture and bake for 10-minutes.
3. Flip chicken thighs over and bake on the other side for an additional 8-minutes

Barbecue Drumsticks

Prep Time: 5 minutes | Cook Time: 20 minutes | Serves 4

- 1 clove garlic, crushed
- Salt and black pepper to taste
- 4 chicken drumsticks
- 1 tablespoon olive oil
- 1 teaspoon chili powder
- ½ tablespoon mustard
- 1 teaspoon liquid Stevia

1. Preheat your air fryer to 390°Fahrenheit. Mix garlic with liquid Stevia, mustard, salt, black pepper, chili powder and oil.
2. Rub drumsticks with marinade and marinate for 20-minutes.
3. Place drumsticks in the air fryer and cook for 10-minutes.
4. Lower the temperature to 300°Fahrenheit and cook for an additional 10-minutes.

Turkey Sliders & Chive Mayonnaise
Prep Time: 5 minutes | Cook Time: 15 minutes | Serves 6

- ¾ lb. turkey mince
- ¼ cup pickled jalapeno, chopped
- 1 tbsp. oyster sauce
- 1 – 2 cloves garlic, minced
- 1 tbsp. chopped fresh cilantro
- 2 tbsp. chopped scallions
- Sea salt and ground black pepper to taste
- 1 cup mayonnaise
- 1 tbsp. chives
- 1 tsp. salt
- Zest of 1 lime

1. In a bowl, combine together all of the ingredients for the turkey sliders. Use your hands to shape 6 equal amounts of the mixture into slider patties.
2. Transfer the patties to the Air Fryer and fry them at 365°F for 15 minutes.
3. In the meantime, prepare the Chive Mayo by combining the rest of the ingredients.
4. Make sandwiches by placing each patty between two burger buns and serve with the mayo.

Dijon Lime Chicken
Prep Time: 3 minutes | Cook Time: 10 minutes | Serves 6

- 8 chicken drumsticks
- 3 tablespoons Dijon mustard
- 1 lime juice
- 1 lime zest
- ¾ teaspoon black pepper
- 1 clove garlic, crushed
- 1 tablespoon light mayonnaise
- 1 tablespoon olive oil
- Salt to taste
- 1 tablespoon parsley, chopped

1. Preheat your air fryer to 375°Fahrenheit. Remove the skin from chicken. Season with salt.
2. In a bowl, mix lime juice, Dijon mustard together. Add lime zest, parsley, garlic, black pepper and mix well. Coat the chicken with lime mixture. Marinate for 15-minutes.
3. Add olive oil to air fryer. Add the chicken drumsticks and cook for 5-minutes. Turn over drumsticks and cook for an additional 5-minutes. Serve hot with mayo.

Cumin Chicken Thighs

Prep Time: 5 minutes | Cook Time: 25 minutes | Serves 4

- 4 chicken thighs, skinless, boneless
- 1 tablespoon coconut oil
- 1 teaspoon ground cumin
- ½ teaspoon salt
- ½ teaspoon smoked paprika

1. Mix chicken thighs with coconut oil, cumin, salt, and smoked paprika.
2. Put the chicken thighs in the air fryer basket and cook at 375F for 25 minutes.

Cauliflower Stuffed Chicken

Prep Time: 20 minutes | Cook Time: 25 minutes | Serves 5

- 1 ½-pound chicken breast, skinless, boneless
- ½ cup cauliflower, shredded
- 1 jalapeno pepper, chopped
- 1 teaspoon ground nutmeg
- 1 teaspoon salt
- ¼ cup Cheddar cheese, shredded
- ½ teaspoon cayenne pepper
- 1 tablespoon cream cheese
- 1 tablespoon sesame oil
- ½ teaspoon dried thyme

1. Make the horizontal cut in the chicken breast. In the mixing bowl mix up shredded cauliflower, chopped jalapeno pepper, ground nutmeg, salt, and cayenne pepper.
2. Fill the chicken cut with the shredded cauliflower and secure the cut with toothpicks. Then rub the chicken breast with cream cheese, dried thyme, and sesame oil.
3. Preheat the air fryer to 380F. Put the chicken breast in the air fryer and cook it for 20 minutes. Then sprinkle it with Cheddar cheese and cook for 5 minutes more.

Pesto Chicken

Prep Time: 10 minutes | Cook Time: 25 minutes | Serves 4

- 1 cup basil pesto
- 2 tablespoons olive oil
- A pinch of salt and black pepper
- 1 and ½ pounds chicken wings

1. In a bowl, mix the chicken wings with all the ingredients and toss well.
2. Put the meat in the air fryer's basket and cook at 380 degrees F for 25 minutes. Divide between plates and serve.

Hoisin Chicken

Prep Time: 25 minutes | Cook Time: 22 minutes | Serves 4

- ½ teaspoon hoisin sauce
- ½ teaspoon salt
- ½ teaspoon chili powder
- ½ teaspoon ground black pepper
- ½ teaspoon ground cumin
- ¼ teaspoon xanthan gum
- 1 teaspoon apple cider vinegar
- 1 tablespoon sesame oil
- 3 tablespoons coconut cream
- ½ teaspoon minced garlic
- ½ teaspoon chili paste
- 1-pound chicken drumsticks
- 2 tablespoons almond flour

1. Rub the chicken drumsticks with salt, chili powder, ground black pepper, ground cumin, and leave for 10 minutes to marinate.
2. Meanwhile, in the mixing bowl mix up chili paste, minced garlic, coconut cream, apple cider vinegar, xanthan gum, and almond flour. Coat the chicken drumsticks in the coconut cream mixture well, and leave to marinate for 10 minutes more.
3. Preheat the air fryer to 375F. Put the chicken drumsticks in the air fryer and cook them for 22 minutes.

Sun-dried Tomatoes and Chicken Mix
Prep Time: 5 minutes | Cook Time: 25 minutes | Serves 4

- 4 chicken thighs, skinless, boneless
- 1 tablespoon olive oil
- A pinch of salt and black pepper
- 1 tablespoon thyme, chopped
- 1 cup chicken stock
- 3 garlic cloves, minced
- ½ cup coconut cream
- 1 cup sun-dried tomatoes, chopped
- 4 tablespoons parmesan, grated

1. Heat up a pan that fits the air fryer with the oil over medium-high heat, add the chicken, salt, pepper and the garlic, and brown for 2-3 minutes on each side.
2. Add the rest of the ingredients except the parmesan, toss, put the pan in the air fryer and cook at 370 degrees F for 20 minutes.
3. Sprinkle the parmesan on top, leave the mix aside for 5 minutes, divide everything between plates and serve.

Cream Cheese Chicken
Prep Time: 10minutes | Cook Time: 25 minutes | Serves 5

- 1 ½-pound chicken breast, skinless, boneless
- 1 teaspoon ground paprika
- ½ teaspoon ground turmeric
- 2 teaspoons cream cheese
- 1 oz scallions, chopped
- 1 teaspoon avocado oil
- ½ teaspoon salt

1. Rub the chicken breast with ground paprika, turmeric, and salt.
2. Then put the chicken in the air fryer basket.
3. Add avocado oil, scallions, and cream cheese.
4. Cook the meal at 375F for 25 minutes.

Ginger Chicken and Lemon Sauce

Prep Time: 5 minutes | **Cook Time:** 25 minutes | **Serves 4**

- 2 tablespoons spring onions, minced
- 1 tablespoon ginger, grated
- 4 garlic cloves, minced
- 2 tablespoons coconut aminos
- 8 chicken drumsticks
- ½ cup chicken stock
- Salt and black pepper to the taste
- 1 teaspoon olive oil
- ¼ cup cilantro, chopped
- 1 tablespoon lemon juice

1. Heat up a pan with the oil over medium-high heat, add the chicken drumsticks, brown them for 2 minutes on each side and transfer to a pan that fits the fryer.
2. Add all the other ingredients, toss everything, put the pan in the fryer and cook at 370 degrees F for 20 minutes.
3. Divide the chicken and lemon sauce between plates and serve.

Air-Fried Hot Wings

Prep Time: 5 minutes | **Cook Time:** 30 minutes | **Serves 6**

- 1 teaspoon liquid Stevia
- 1 tablespoon Worcestershire sauce
- ½ cup butter, melted
- 4 lbs. chicken wings
- ½ cup hot sauce
- ½ teaspoon salt

1. Add Stevia, Worcestershire sauce, butter, salt, and hot sauce in a bowl and mix well. Set aside.
2. Place chicken wings in air fryer basket and air fry at 380°Fahrenheit for 25-minutes. Shake basket halfway through.
3. After 25-minutes, change the temperature to 400°Fahrenheit for 5-minutes. Add air-fried chicken wings into bowl mixture and toss well.

Keto TSO Chicken
Prep Time: 25 minutes | Cook Time: 22 minutes | Serves 4

- 1-pound chicken breast, skinless, boneless, chopped
- 1 tablespoon avocado oil
- 1 teaspoon ground black pepper
- 1 teaspoon salt
- 1 tablespoon coconut aminos
- ½ cup almond flour
- 1 teaspoon Erythritol
- 1 chili pepper, chopped
- 2 oz scallions, chopped
- 1 teaspoon coconut oil
- ¼ cup of water

1. Rub the chicken with avocado oil, ground black pepper, salt, and coconut aminos/
2. Add water and leave the chicken for 15 minutes to marinate.
3. Meanwhile, mix almond flour with Erythritol, chili pepper, and scallions.
4. Coat the chicken in the almond flour mixture and put it in the air fryer. Add coconut oil.
5. Cook the meal at 375F for 11 minutes per side.

Jalapeno Chicken Drumsticks
Prep Time: 5 minutes | Cook Time: 25 minutes | Serves 4

- 2-pound chicken drumsticks
- 2 jalapeno peppers, minced
- 1 tablespoon avocado oil
- 1 teaspoon ground black pepper
- ½ teaspoon garlic powder

1. In the mixing bowl mix chicken drumsticks with jalapeno peppers, avocado oil, ground black pepper, and garlic powder.
2. Put the chicken drumsticks in the air fryer and cook at 370F for 25 minutes.

Chicken Quesadilla Melt
Prep Time: 15 minutes | Cook Time: 10 minutes | Serves 2

- 2 keto tortillas
- 9 oz chicken fillet, cooked, shredded
- 1 jalapeno pepper, sliced
- 3 oz Parmesan, grated
- 1 teaspoon dried dill

1. In the mixing bowl, mix shredded chicken with jalapeno pepper, Parmesan, and dried dill.
2. Then spread the mixture over the tortillas and fold them.
3. Put the tortillas in the air fryer basket and cook at 390F for 5 minutes per side.

Provolone Chicken Breasts
Prep Time: 5 minutes | Cook Time: 24 minutes | Serves 6

- 3-pounds chicken breast, skinless, boneless
- 1 tablespoon coconut oil
- 5 oz provolone cheese, shredded
- 1 teaspoon dried oregano
- 1 teaspoon dried cilantro

1. Rub the chicken breast with dried oregano and cilantro.
2. Then brush the chicken breast with coconut oil and put it in the air fryer basket.
3. Cook it for 20 minutes at 385F.
4. Then top the chicken breast with Provolone cheese and cook the meal for 4 minutes more.

Chapter 4
Beef, Lamb and Pork

Beef & Mushrooms

Prep Time: 3 hours | Cook Time: 15 minutes | Serves 1

- 6 oz. beef
- ¼ onion, diced
- ½ cup mushroom slices
- 2 tbsp. favorite marinade

1. Slice or cube the beef and put it in a bowl.
2. Cover the meat with the marinade, place a layer of aluminum foil or saran wrap over the bowl, and place the bowl in the refrigerator for 3 hours.
3. Put the meat in a baking dish along with the onion and mushrooms
4. Air Fry at 350°F for 10 minutes. Serve hot.

Max's Meatloaf

Prep Time: 5 minutes | Cook Time: 30 minutes | Serves 4

- 1 large onion, peeled and diced
- 2 kg. minced beef
- 1 tsp. Worcester sauce
- 3 tbsp. tomato ketchup
- 1 tbsp. basil
- 1 tbsp. oregano
- 1 tbsp. mixed herbs
- 1 tbsp. friendly bread crumbs
- Salt & pepper to taste

1. In a large bowl, combine the mince with the herbs, Worcester sauce, onion and tomato ketchup, incorporating every component well.
2. Pour in the breadcrumbs and give it another stir.
3. Transfer the mixture to a small dish and cook for 25 minutes in the Air Fryer at 350°F.

Air-Fried Lamb Chops
Prep Time: 5 minutes | Cook Time: 32 minutes | Serves 4

- 1 tablespoon + 2 tablespoons
- olive oil, divided
- 4 lamb chops
- Pinch of black pepper
- 1 tablespoon dried thyme
- 1 garlic clove

1. Preheat your air fryer to 390°Fahrenheit. Cook the garlic with 1 teaspoon olive oil for 10-minutes in air fryer.
2. Combine thyme and pepper with rest of olive oil. Squeeze the roasted garlic and stir into thyme and oil mixture. Brush mixture over lamb chops. Cook for 12-minutes in air fryer.

Roasted Rack of Lamb with Macadamia Crust
Prep Time: 5 minutes | Cook Time: 35 minutes | Serves 4

- 1 garlic clove, minced
- 1 1/3 lbs. rack of lamb
- 1 tablespoon olive oil
- Salt and pepper to taste
- 3-ounces macadamia nuts, raw and unsalted
- 1 egg, beaten
- 1 tablespoon fresh rosemary, chopped
- 1 tablespoon breadcrumbs

1. In a small mixing bowl, mix garlic and olive oil. Brush all over lamb and season with salt and pepper.
2. In your food processor, chop macadamia nuts and mix with breadcrumbs and rosemary. Be careful not to make the nuts into a paste. Stir in egg. Coat lamb with nut mixture.
3. Preheat your air fryer to 220°Fahrenheit. Place the lamb in air fryer and cook for 30-minutes. Raise the temperature to 390°Fahrenheit and cook for an additional 5-minutes.
4. Remove the meat, cover it loosely with foil for 10-minutes. Serve warm.

Onion Carrot Meatloaf
Prep Time: 5 minutes | Cook Time: 25 minutes | Serves 6

- 1 lb. ground beef
- Salt and pepper to taste
- ½ cup breadcrumbs
- ¼ cup milk
- ½ onion, shredded
- 2 carrots, shredded
- 1 egg

1. Preheat your air fryer to 400°Fahrenheit. Mix all your ingredients in a bowl. Add the meatloaf mixture to a loaf pan and place it in your air fryer basket. Cook in air fryer for 25-minutes and serve warm.

Pork Satay with Peanut Sauce
Prep Time: 5 minutes | Cook Time: 21 minutes | Serves 4

- 1 teaspoon ground ginger
- 2 teaspoons hot pepper sauce
- 2 cloves garlic, crushed
- 3 tablespoons sweet soy sauce
- 3 ½ ounces unsalted peanuts, ground
- ¾ cup coconut milk
- 1 teaspoon ground coriander
- 2 tablespoons vegetable oil
- 14-ounces lean pork chops, in cubes of 1-inch

1. In a large mixing bowl, combine hot sauce, ginger, half garlic, oil and soy sauce. Place the meat into the mixture and leave for 15-minutes to marinate.
2. Place the meat into wire basket of your air fryer. Cook at 390°Fahrenheit for 12-minutes. Turn over halfway through cook time.
3. For the peanut sauce, place the oil into a skillet and heat it up. Add the garlic and coriander and cook for 5-minutes, stirring often.
4. Add the coconut milk, peanuts, hot pepper sauce and soy sauce to the pan and bring to boil. Stir often.
5. Remove the pork from air fryer and pour sauce over it and serve warm.

Cheese Burgers
Prep Time: 3 minutes | Cook Time: 11 minutes | Serves 6

- 1 lb. ground beef
- 6 slices cheddar cheese
- Salt and pepper to taste

1. Preheat the air fryer to 350°Fahrenheit. Season ground beef with pepper and salt. Make six patties from the mixture and place them into air fryer basket. Air fry patties for 10-minutes.
2. After 10-minutes, place cheese slices over patties and cook for another minute. Serve warm.

Meatballs with Sauce
Prep Time: 3 minutes | Cook Time: 12 minutes | Serves 8

- 1 lb. ground beef
- 1 egg, beaten
- 1 cup tomato sauce
- Salt and pepper to taste
- 1 small onion, minced
- ½ cup breadcrumbs
- 2 carrots, shredded
- ½ teaspoon garlic salt

1. Preheat air fryer to 400°Fahrenheit. Mix egg, carrots, breadcrumbs, onion, ground beef, garlic salt, salt, and pepper. Mix well. Make small meatballs out of mixture and place in the air fryer basket for 7 minutes.
2. Place meatballs in oven safe dish and pour tomato sauce over meatballs. Place the dish in the air fryer and cook at 320°Fahrenheit for 5-minutes. Serve warm.

Spicy Beef Schnitzel
Prep Time: 5 minutes | Cook Time: 12 minutes | Serves 4

- 4 thin beef schnitzels
- 2 tablespoons paprika
- 1 cup breadcrumbs
- 1 tablespoon sesame seeds
- 2 eggs, beaten
- 4 tablespoons almond flour
- 3 tablespoons olive oil
- Salt and pepper to taste

1. Preheat the air fryer to 350°Fahrenheit. Season schnitzel with pepper and salt. In a bowl, mix the flour, salt, and paprika.
2. In another bowl, mix breadcrumbs, olive oil, and sesame seeds. Add beaten eggs into a third bowl. Dip the schnitzel into flour mixture, then into the egg, and finally coat with breadcrumbs. Place coated schnitzel in air fryer basket and cook for 12-minutes. Serve warm.

Dijon Pork Chops
Prep Time: 10 minutes | Cook Time: 20 minutes | Serves 4

- 4 pork chops
- 1 tablespoon Dijon mustard
- 1 teaspoon chili powder
- 1 tablespoon avocado oil

1. Mix Dijon mustard with chili powder and avocado oil.
2. Then carefully brush the pork chops with the mustard mixture from both sides.
3. Cook the pork chops at 375F for 10 minutes per side.

Pumpkin & Pork Empanadas

Prep Time: 5 minutes | Cook Time: 30 minutes | Serves 4

- 2 tablespoons olive oil
- 1 package of 10 empanada discs
- Black pepper to taste
- 1 teaspoon salt
- ½ teaspoon dried thyme
- ½ teaspoon cinnamon
- 1 red chili pepper, minced
- 3 tablespoons water
- 1 ½ cups pumpkin puree
- 1 lb. ground pork
- ½ onion, diced

1. In a saucepan warm some olive oil. Fry the onions and pork for about 5-minutes.
2. Pour away the fat, then add pumpkin, chili, cinnamon, water, thyme, salt, and pepper. Stir well. Cook for 10-minutes to allow flavors to blend. Set aside to cool.
3. Open the packet of empanada discs and spread them out over your countertop. Add a couple of tablespoons of filling to each, brush the edges with water and then fold towards center, to form a Cornish pasty shape. Brush olive oil and repeat with the rest. Place the empanadas inside of wire basket in your air fryer and cook at 370°Fahrenheit for 15-minutes. Make sure to check often and turn as required. Serve and enjoy!

Coconut Pork and Green Beans

Prep Time: 5 minutes | Cook Time: 25 minutes | Serves 4

- 4 pork chops
- 2 tablespoons coconut oil, melted
- 2 garlic cloves, minced
- A pinch of salt and black pepper
- ½ pound green beans, trimmed and halved
- 2 tablespoons keto tomato sauce

1. Heat up a pan that fits the air fryer with the oil over medium heat, add the pork chops and brown for 5 minutes.
2. Add the rest of the ingredients, put the pan in the machine and cook at 390 degrees F for 20 minutes.
3. Divide everything between plates and serve

Italian Pork

Prep Time: 10 minutes | Cook Time: 50 minutes | Serves 2

- 8 oz pork loin
- 1 tablespoon sesame oil
- ½ teaspoon salt
- 1 teaspoon Italian herbs

1. In the shallow bowl mix up Italian herbs, salt, and sesame oil. Then brush the pork loin with the Italian herbs mixture and wrap in the foil.
2. Preheat the air fryer to 350F. Put the wrapped pork loin in the air fryer and cook it for 50 minutes. When the time is over, remove the meat from the air fryer and discard the foil. Slice the pork loin into the servings.

Chili Tomato Pork

Prep Time: 15 minutes | Cook Time: 15 minutes | Serves 3

- 12 oz pork tenderloin
- 1 tablespoon grain mustard
- 1 tablespoon swerve
- 1 tablespoon keto tomato sauce
- 1 teaspoon chili pepper, grinded
- ¼ teaspoon garlic powder
- 1 tablespoon olive oil

1. In the mixing bowl mix up grain mustard, swerve, tomato sauce, chili pepper, garlic powder, and olive oil. Rub the pork tenderloin with mustard mixture generously and leave for 5-10 minutes to marinate. Meanwhile, preheat the air fryer to 370F.
2. Put the marinated pork tenderloin in the air fryer baking pan. Then insert the baking pan in the preheated air fryer and cook the meat for 15 minutes.
3. Cool the cooked meat to the room temperature and slice it into the servings.

Greek Pork and Spinach
Prep Time: 5 minutes | Cook Time: 25 minutes | Serves 4

- 2 pounds pork tenderloin, cut into strips
- 2 tablespoons coconut oil, melted
- A pinch of salt and black pepper
- 6 ounces baby spinach
- 1 cup cherry tomatoes, halved
- 1 cup feta cheese, crumbled

1. Heat up a pan that fits your air fryer with the oil over medium high heat, add the pork and brown for 5 minutes.
2. Add the rest of the ingredients except the spinach and the cheese, put the pan to your air fryer, cook at 390 degrees F for 15 minutes.
3. Add the spinach, toss, and cook for 5 minutes more.
4. Divide between plates and serve with feta cheese sprinkled on top.

Pork and Asparagus
Prep Time: 5 minutes | Cook Time: 35 minutes | Serves 4

- 2 pounds pork loin, boneless and cubed
- ¾ cup beef stock
- 2 tablespoons olive oil
- 3 tablespoons keto tomato sauce
- 1 pound asparagus, trimmed and halved
- ½ tablespoon oregano, chopped
- Salt and black pepper to the taste

1. Heat up a pan that fits your air fryer with the oil over medium heat, add the pork, toss and brown for 5 minutes.
2. Add the rest of the ingredients, toss a bit, put the pan in the fryer and cook at 380 degrees F for 30 minutes.
3. Divide everything between plates and serve.

Pork Stuffing
Prep Time: 10minutes | Cook Time: 35 minutes | Serves 6

- 4 oz pork rinds
- 2 pecans, chopped
- 1 teaspoon Italian seasonings
- ½ teaspoon white pepper
- 1 egg, beaten
- 4 tablespoons almond flour
- 3 cups ground pork
- 1 tablespoon avocado oil
- ¼ cup heavy cream

1. Put all ingredients in the mixing bowl and stir until homogenous.
2. Then transfer the mixture in the air fryer and cook it at 360F for 35 minutes.
3. Stir the meal every 10 minutes.

African Style Pork Shoulder
Prep Time: 25 minutes | Cook Time: 50 minutes | Serves 4

- 2-pound pork shoulder
- 1 teaspoon dried sage
- 1 teaspoon curry powder
- ¼ cup plain yogurt
- 1 tablespoon avocado oil

1. Mix curry powder with plain yogurt and avocado oil.
2. Add dried sage and stir the mixture.
3. Then brush the pork shoulder with plain yogurt mixture and leave for 20 minutes to marinate.
4. Then transfer the pork shoulder in the air fryer. Add all remaining yogurt mixture.
5. Cook the meal at 365F for 50 minutes.

Scallions Pork Chops
Prep Time: 25 minutes | Cook Time: 20 minutes | Serves 4

- 2 tablespoons avocado oil
- 4 pork chops
- 2 oz scallions, minced
- 1 teaspoon onion powder

1. In the shallow bowl mix avocado oil with minced scallions and onion powder.
2. Then mix scallions mixture with pork chops and leave for 10-15 minutes to marinate.

Chapter 5
Fish and Seafood

Cod Fish Teriyaki with Oysters, Mushrooms & Veggies
Prep Time: 3 minutes | Cook Time: 10 minutes | Serves 2

- 1 tablespoon olive oil
- 6 pieces mini king oyster
- mushrooms, thinly sliced
- 2 slices (1-inch) codfish
- 1 Napa cabbage leaf, sliced
- 1 clove garlic, chopped
- Salt to taste
- 1 green onion, minced
- Veggies, steamed of your choice
- 1 teaspoon liquid stevia
- 2 tablespoons mirin
- 2 tablespoons soy sauce

1. Prepare teriyaki sauce by mixing all the ingredients in a bowl then set aside. Grease the air fryer basket with oil. Place the mushrooms, garlic, Napa cabbage leaf, and salt inside. Layer the fish on top. Preheat your air fryer to 360°Fahrenheit for 3-minutes.
2. Place the basket in air fryer and cook for 5-minutes. Stir. Pour the teriyaki sauce over ingredients in the basket. Cook for an additional 5-minutes. Serve with your choice of steamed veggies.

Crab Buns
Prep Time: 15 minutes | Cook Time: 20 minutes | Serves 2

- 5 oz crab meat, chopped
- 2 eggs, beaten
- 2 tablespoons coconut flour
- ¼ teaspoon baking powder
- ½ teaspoon coconut aminos
- ½ teaspoon ground black pepper
- 1 tablespoon coconut oil, softened

1. In the mixing bowl, mix crab meat with eggs, coconut flour, baking powder, coconut aminos, ground black pepper, and coconut oil.
2. Knead the smooth dough and cut it into pieces.
3. Make the buns from the crab mixture and put them in the air fryer basket.
4. Cook the crab buns at 365F for 20 minutes.

Salmon with Dill Sauce
Prep Time: 5 minutes | Cook Time: 23 minutes | Serves 4

- 1½ lbs. of salmon
- 4 teaspoons olive oil
- Pinch of sea salt
- ½ cup non-fat Greek yogurt
- ½ cup light sour cream
- 2 tablespoons dill, finely chopped
- Pinch of sea salt

1. Preheat your air fryer to 270°Fahrenheit. Cut salmon into four 6-ounce portions and drizzle 1 teaspoon of olive oil over each piece. Season with sea salt. Place salmon into cooking basket and cook for 23-minutes.
2. Make dill sauce. In a mixing bowl, mix sour cream, yogurt, chopped dill and sea salt. Top cooked salmon with sauce and garnish with additional dill and serve.

Grilled Salmon with Capers & Dill
Prep Time: 2 minutes | Cook Time: 8 minutes | Serves 2

- 1 teaspoon capers, chopped
- 2 sprigs dill, chopped
- 1 lemon zest
- 1 tablespoon olive oil
- 4 slices lemon (optional)
- 11-ounce salmon fillet
- 5 capers, chopped
- 1 sprig dill, chopped
- 2 tablespoons plain yogurt
- Pinch of lemon zest
- Salt and black pepper to taste

1. Preheat your air fryer to 400°Fahrenheit. Mix dill, capers, lemon zest, olive oil and salt in a bowl. Cover the salmon with this mixture. Cook salmon for 8-minutes.
2. Combine the dressing ingredients in another bowl. When salmon is cooked, place on serving plate and drizzle dressing over it. Place lemon slices at the side of the plate and serve.

Stevia Cod

Prep Time: 5 minutes | Cook Time: 14 minutes | Serves 4

- 1/3 cup stevia
- 2 tablespoons coconut aminos
- 4 cod fillets, boneless
- A pinch of salt and black pepper

1. In a pan that fits the air fryer, combine all the ingredients and toss gently. Introduce the pan in the fryer and cook at 350 degrees F for 14 minutes, flipping the fish halfway.
2. Divide everything between plates and serve.

Butter Crab Muffins

Prep Time: 15 minutes | Cook Time: 20 minutes | Serves 2

- 5 oz crab meat, chopped
- 2 eggs, beaten
- 2 tablespoons almond flour
- ¼ teaspoon baking powder
- ½ teaspoon apple cider vinegar
- ½ teaspoon ground paprika
- 1 tablespoon butter, softened
- Cooking spray

1. Grind the chopped crab meat and put it in the bowl. Add eggs, almond flour, baking powder, apple cider vinegar, ground paprika, and butter. Stir the mixture until homogenous.
2. Preheat the air fryer to 365F. Spray the muffin molds with cooking spray. Then pour the crab meat batter in the muffin molds and place them in the preheated air fryer. Cook the crab muffins for 20 minutes or until they are light brown.
3. Cool the cooked muffins to the room temperature and remove from the muffin mold.

Tilapia and Kale
Prep Time: 5 minutes | Cook Time: 20 minutes | Serves 4

- 4 tilapia fillets, boneless
- Salt and black pepper to the taste
- 2 garlic cloves, minced
- 1 teaspoon fennel seeds
- ½ teaspoon red pepper flakes, crushed
- 1 bunch kale, chopped
- 3 tablespoons olive oil

1. In a pan that fits the fryer, combine all the ingredients, put the pan in the fryer and cook at 360 degrees F for 20 minutes.
2. Divide everything between plates and serve.

Air-Fried Asian Style Fish
Prep Time: 20 minutes | Cook Time: 20 minutes | Serves 2

- 1 medium sea bass
- or halibut (12-ounces)
- 2 garlic cloves, minced
- 1 tablespoon olive oil
- 3 slices of ginger, julienned
- 2 tablespoons cooking wine
- 1 tomato, cut into quarters
- 1 lime, thinly cut
- 1 green onion, chopped
- 1 chili, diced

1. Prepare ginger, garlic oil mixture: sauté ginger and garlic with oil until golden brown in a small saucepan over medium-heat on top of the stove. Preheat your air fryer to 360°Fahrenheit. Prepare fish: clean, rinse, and pat dry. Cut in half to fit into air fryer.
2. Place the fish inside of air fryer basket then drizzle it with cooking wine. Layer tomato and lime slices on top of fish. Cover with garlic ginger oil mixture. Top with green onion and slices of chili. Cover with aluminum foil. Cook for 20-minutes.

Chili Haddock

Prep Time: 10 minutes | Cook Time: 8 minutes | Serves 4

- 12 oz haddock fillet
- 1 egg, beaten
- 1 teaspoon cream cheese
- 1 teaspoon chili flakes
- ½ teaspoon salt
- 1 tablespoon flax meal
- Cooking spray

1. Cut the haddock on 4 pieces and sprinkle with chili flakes and salt. After this, in the small bowl mix up egg and cream cheese. Dip the haddock pieces in the egg mixture and generously sprinkle with flax meal.
2. Preheat the air fryer to 400F. Put the prepared haddock pieces in the air fryer in one layer and cook them for 4 minutes from each side or until they are golden brown.

Rosemary Shrimp Skewers

Prep Time: 10 minutes | Cook Time: 5 minutes | Serves 5

- 4-pounds shrimps, peeled
- 1 tablespoon dried rosemary
- 1 tablespoon avocado oil
- 1 teaspoon apple cider vinegar

1. Mix the shrimps with dried rosemary, avocado oil, and apple cider vinegar.
2. Then sting the shrimps into skewers and put in the air fryer.
3. Cook the shrimps at 400F for 5 minutes.

Black Cod with Grapes, Pecans, Fennel & Kale
Prep Time: 3 minutes | Cook Time: 15 minutes | Serves 2

- 2 fillets black cod (8-ounces)
- 3 cups kale, minced
- 2 teaspoons white balsamic vinegar
- ½ cup pecans
- 1 cup grapes, halved
- 1 small bulb fennel, cut into inch-thick slices
- 4 tablespoons extra-virgin olive oil
- Salt and black pepper to taste

1. Preheat your air fryer to 400°Fahrenheit. Use salt and pepper to season your fish fillets. Drizzle with 1 teaspoon of olive oil. Place the fish inside of air fryer with the skin side down and cook for 10-minutes.
2. Take the fish out and cover loosely with aluminum foil. Combine fennel, pecans, and grapes. Pour 2 tablespoons of olive oil and season with salt and pepper. Add to the air fryer basket. Cook for an additional 5-minutes.
3. In a bowl combine minced kale and cooked grapes, fennel and pecans. Cover ingredients with balsamic vinegar and remaining 1 tablespoon of olive oil. Toss gently. Serve fish with sauce and enjoy!

Sweet Tilapia Fillets
Prep Time: 5 minutes | Cook Time: 14 minutes | Serves 4

- 2 tablespoons Erythritol
- 1 tablespoon apple cider vinegar
- 4 tilapia fillets, boneless
- 1 teaspoon olive oil

1. Mix apple cider vinegar with olive oil and Erythritol.
2. Then rub the tilapia fillets with the sweet mixture and put in the air fryer basket in one layer.
3. Cook the fish at 360F for 7 minutes per side.

Chili and Oregano Tilapia
Prep Time: 5 minutes | Cook Time: 20 minutes | Serves 4

- 4 tilapia fillets, boneless
- 1 teaspoon chili flakes
- 1 teaspoon dried oregano
- 1 tablespoon avocado oil
- 1 teaspoon mustard

1. Rub the tilapia fillets with chili flakes, dried oregano, avocado oil, and mustard and put in the air fryer.
2. Cook it for 10 minutes per side at 360F.

Chapter 6
Vegetarian Recipes

Cumin, Chili & Squash
Prep Time: 5 minutes | Cook Time: 20 minutes | Serves 4

- 1 medium butternut squash
- 1 bunch coriander
- 2/3 cup Greek yogurt
- ¼ cup pine nuts
- 1 tablespoon olive oil
- 1 pinch chili flakes
- 2 teaspoons cumin seeds
- Salt and pepper to taste

1. Slice the squash into small chunks. Mix with the spices and oil in a baking pan. Roast the squash in your air fryer at 380°Fahrenheit for 20-minutes.
2. Toast the pine nuts and serve with Greek yogurt and sprinkle coriander on top.

Pineapple Sticks with Yogurt Dip
Prep Time: 3 minutes | Cook Time: 10 minutes | Serves 2

- ¼ cup dried coconut
- ½ pineapple
- 1 cup vanilla yogurt
- 1 sprig of fresh mint

1. Preheat your air fryer to 390°Fahrenheit. Cut the pineapple into sticks. Dip pineapple sticks into the dried coconut. Place the sticks covered with desiccated coconut into air fryer basket and cook for 10-minutes.
2. Prepare the yogurt dip. Dice the mint leaves and combine with vanilla yogurt and stir. Serve pineapple sticks with yogurt dip and enjoy!

Low-Carb Zucchini Roll-Ups
Prep Time: 5 minutes | Cook Time: 5 minutes | Serves 2

- 3 zucchinis, sliced thin, lengthwise
- Sea salt to taste
- 1 cup goat cheese
- ¼ teaspoon black pepper
- 1 tablespoon olive oil

1. Preheat air fryer to 390°Fahrenheit. Brush each zucchini strip with olive oil. Mix sea salt and black pepper with goat cheese. Spoon the goat cheese into the middle of each strip of zucchini and roll it up and fasten with a toothpick.
2. Place into air fryer and cook for 5-minutes.

Coconut Broccoli
Prep Time: 5 minutes | Cook Time: 30 minutes | Serves 4

- 3 tablespoons ghee, melted
- 15 ounces coconut cream
- 2 eggs, whisked
- 2 cups cheddar, grated
- 1 cup parmesan, grated
- 1 tablespoon mustard
- 1 pound broccoli florets
- A pinch of salt and black pepper
- 1 tablespoon parsley, chopped

1. Grease a baking pan that fits the air fryer with the ghee and arrange the broccoli on the bottom. Add the cream, mustard, salt, pepper and the eggs and toss. Sprinkle the cheese on top, put the pan in the air fryer and cook at 380 degrees F for 30 minutes.
2. Divide between plates and serve.

Broccoli and Cranberries Mix

Prep Time: 5 minutes | Cook Time: 25 minutes | Serves 4

- 1 broccoli head, florets separated
- 2 shallots, chopped
- A pinch of salt and black pepper
- ½ cup cranberries
- ½ cup almonds, chopped
- 6 bacon slices, cooked and crumbled
- 3 tablespoons balsamic vinegar

1. In a pan that fits the air fryer, combine the broccoli with the rest of the ingredients and toss. Put the pan in the air fryer and cook at 380 degrees F for 25 minutes. Divide between plates and serve.

Zucchini Fries & Roasted Garlic Aioli

Prep Time: 5 minutes | Cook Time: 12 minutes | Serves 4

- ½ cup mayonnaise
- Sea salt and pepper to taste
- 1 teaspoon roasted garlic, pureed
- 2 tablespoons olive oil
- ½ lemon, juiced
- Sea salt and pepper to taste
- ½ cup almond flour
- 2 eggs, beaten
- 1 cup breadcrumbs
- 1 large zucchini, cut into ½-inch sticks
- 1 tablespoon olive oil
- Cooking spray

1. Take three bowls and line them up on the counter. In the first, combine flour, salt, and pepper. Place eggs in the second bowl. Place breadcrumbs combined with salt and pepper in the third bowl. Take zucchini sticks and dip first into flour, then in the eggs, and then into crumbs. Preheat your air fryer to 400°Fahrenheit.
2. Cover sticks with cooking spray and layer in the basket. There should be two layers, pointing in opposite directions. Halfway through the 12-minute cook time rotate and turn the fries and spray with more cooking spray. Prepare the roasted garlic aioli in a medium bowl by mixing mayonnaise, pureed roasted garlic, olive oil and lemon juice. Stir in some pepper and salt. Serve the fries with the roasted garlic aioli and enjoy!

Coconut Kohlrabi Mash
Prep Time: 10 minutes | Cook Time: 20 minutes | Serves 6

- 12 oz kohlrabi, chopped
- 2 tablespoons coconut cream
- 1 teaspoon salt
- ½ cup Monterey Jack cheese, shredded
- ¼ cup chicken broth
- ½ teaspoon chili flakes

1. In the air fryer pan mix up kohlrabi, coconut cream, salt, Monterey jack cheese, chicken broth, and chili flakes. Then preheat the air fryer to 255F. Cook the meal for 20 minutes.

Roasted Kabocha Squash
Prep Time: 10 minutes | Cook Time: 12 minutes | Serves 4

- 10 oz Kabocha squash
- 1 teaspoon onion powder
- 1 oz scallions, chopped
- 1 tablespoon olive oil
- ½ teaspoon chili flakes

1. Cut the squash into cubes and sprinkle with onion powder, olive oil, and chili flakes.
2. Put the kabocha squash in the air fryer and cook at 365F for 6 minutes per side.
3. Top the cooked meal with scallions.

Broccoli and Scallions Sauce
Prep Time: 5 minutes | Cook Time: 15 minutes | Serves 4

- 1 broccoli head, florets separated
- Salt and black pepper to the taste
- ½ cup keto tomato sauce
- 1 tablespoon sweet paprika
- ¼ cup scallions, chopped
- 1 tablespoon olive oil

1. In a pan that fits the air fryer, combine the broccoli with the rest of the ingredients, toss, put the pan in the fryer and cook at 380 degrees F for 15 minutes.
2. Divide between plates and serve.

Zucchini and Squash Mix
Prep Time: 15 minutes | Cook Time: 12 minutes | Serves 4

- 10 oz Kabocha squash
- ½ zucchini, chopped
- 3 spring onions, chopped
- 1 teaspoon dried thyme
- 2 teaspoons ghee
- 1 teaspoon salt
- 1 teaspoon ground turmeric

1. Chop the squash into small cubes and sprinkle with salt and ground turmeric. Put the squash in the bowl, add zucchini, spring onions, dried thyme, and ghee. Shake the vegetables gently.
2. Preheat the air fryer to 400F. Put the vegetable mixture in the air fryer and cook for 12 minutes. Shake the vegetables after 6 minutes of cooking to avoid burning.

Zucchini, Carrots & Yellow Squash
Prep Time: 5 minutes | Cook Time: 35 minutes | Serves 4

- ½ lb carrots, diced
- 1 lime, cut into wedges
- ½ teaspoon ground white pepper
- 1 lb. zucchini, trim stem and root ends, cut into ¾ inch semicircles
- 1 lb. yellow squash, with roots and stems, trimmed
- 6 teaspoons olive oil, divided
- 1 teaspoon sea salt
- 1 tablespoon tarragon leaves, chopped

1. In a bowl add carrots and cover with 2 teaspoons of oil and stir. Put the carrots in fryer basket and set to 400°Fahrenheit and cook for 5-minutes.
2. Place the zucchini and yellow squash into a bowl. Cover with the remaining 4 teaspoons of olive oil. Season with pepper and salt. When air fryer timer goes off, stir in zucchini and yellow squash with carrots. Cook for 30-minutes. Stir from time to time. Garnish with lime wedges and tarragon leaves.

Cauliflower Casserole
Prep Time: 10 minutes | Cook Time: 30 minutes | Serves 4

- 3 tablespoons coconut oil, melted
- 1 cup heavy cream
- 2 eggs, beaten
- 2 cups Monterey Jack cheese, shredded
- 2 cups cauliflower, chopped
- 1 teaspoon dried cilantro

1. Mix cauliflower with coconut oil and put in the air fryer basket in one layer.
2. Then top the vegetables with cilantro and cheese.
3. Then mix heavy cream with eggs and pour the liquid over the cheese.
4. Cook the casserole at 360F for 30 minutes.

Vinegar Cauliflower Mix
Prep Time: 5 minutes | Cook Time: 25 minutes | Serves 4

- 1-pound cauliflower, chopped
- 2 oz spring onions, chopped
- ½ teaspoon white pepper
- 4 oz prosciutto, chopped
- 1 pecan, chopped
- 3 tablespoons apple cider vinegar
- 1 tablespoon avocado oil

1. Put all ingredients in the air fryer basket and carefully mix.
2. Cook the meal at 360F for 25 minutes.

Chapter 7
Desserts and Staples

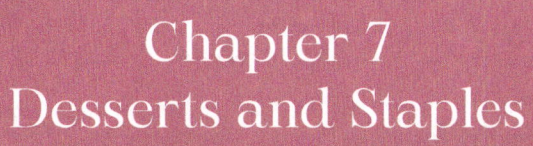

Banana Oatmeal Cookies

Prep Time: 5 minutes | Cook Time: 20 minutes | Serves 6

- 2 cups quick oats
- 4 ripe bananas, mashed
- ¼ cup coconut, shredded

1. Preheat the Air Fryer to 350°F.
2. Combine all of the ingredients in a bowl.
3. Scoop equal amounts of the cookie dough onto a baking sheet and put it in the Air Fryer basket.
4. Bake the cookies for 15 minutes.

Sweet & Crisp Bananas

Prep Time: 3 minutes | Cook Time: 20 minutes | Serves 4

- 4 ripe bananas, peeled and halved
- 1 tbsp. meal
- 1 tbsp. cashew, crushed
- 1 egg, beaten
- 1½ tbsp. coconut oil
- ¼ cup flour
- 1½ tbsp. sugar
- ½ cup friendly bread crumbs

1. Put the coconut oil in a saucepan and heat over a medium heat. Stir in the bread crumbs and cook, stirring continuously, for 4 minutes.
2. Transfer the bread crumbs to a bowl.
3. Coat each of the banana halves in the corn flour, before dipping it in the beaten egg and lastly coating it with the bread crumbs.
4. Put the coated banana halves in the Air Fryer basket. Season with the sugar.
5. Air fry at 350°F for 10 minutes.

Coconut Prune Cookies

Prep Time: 5 minutes | Cook Time: 20 minutes | Serves 10

- ½ teaspoon baking soda
- ½ teaspoon baking powder
- ½ teaspoon orange zest
- 1 teaspoon vanilla paste
- 1/3 teaspoon ground cinnamon
- 1 stick butter, softened
- 1½ cups almond flour
- 2 tablespoons Truvia for baking
- 1/3 cup prunes, chopped
- 1/3 coconut, shredded

1. Mix the butter with Truvia until mixture becomes fluffy; sift in the flour and add baking powder, as well as baking soda. Add the remaining ingredients and combine well. Knead the dough and transfer it to the fridge for 20-minutes.
2. To finish, shape the chilled dough into bite-size balls; arrange the balls on a baking dish and gently flatten them with the back of a spoon. Air-fry for 20-minutes at 315°Fahrenheit.

Delicious Clafoutis

Prep Time: 5 minutes | Cook Time: 25 minutes | Serves 6

- ¼ teaspoon nutmeg, grated
- ½ teaspoon crystalized ginger
- 1/3 teaspoon ground cinnamon
- ½ teaspoon baking soda
- ½ teaspoon baking powder
- 2 tablespoons Truvia for baking
- ½ cup coconut cream
- ¾ cup coconut milk
- 3 eggs, whisked
- 4 medium-sized pears, cored and sliced
- 1½ cups plums, pitted
- ¾ cup almond flour

1. Lightly grease 2 mini pie pans using a non-stick cooking spray. Lay the plums and pears on the bottom of pie pans. In a saucepan that is preheated over medium heat, warm the cream along with the coconut milk until thoroughly heated. Remove the pan from heat; mix in the flour along with baking soda and baking powder.
2. In a bowl, mix the eggs, Truvia, spices until the mixture is creamy. Add the creamy milk mixture. Carefully spread this mixture over your fruit in pans. Bake at 320°Fahrenheit for 25-minutes.

Pear & Apple Crisp with Walnuts

Prep Time: 5 minutes | Cook Time: 25 minutes | Serves 6

- ½ lb. apples, cored and chopped
- ½ lb. pears, cored and chopped
- 1 cup flour
- 1 cup sugar
- 1 tbsp. butter
- 1 tsp. ground cinnamon
- ¼ tsp. ground cloves
- 1 tsp. vanilla extract
- ¼ cup chopped walnuts
- Whipped cream, to serve

1. Lightly grease a baking dish and place the apples and pears inside.
2. Combine the rest of the ingredients, minus the walnuts and the whipped cream, until a coarse, crumbly texture is achieved.
3. Pour the mixture over the fruits and spread it evenly. Top with the chopped walnuts.
4. Air bake at 340°F for 20 minutes or until the top turns golden brown.
5. When cooked through, serve at room temperature with whipped cream.

Lemon Pie

Prep Time: 10 minutes | Cook Time: 35 minutes | Serves 8

- 2 eggs, whisked
- ¾ cup swerve
- ¼ cup coconut flour
- 2 tablespoons butter, melted
- 1 teaspoon lemon zest, grated
- 1 teaspoon baking powder
- 1 teaspoon vanilla extract
- ½ teaspoon lemon extract
- 4 ounces coconut, shredded
- Cooking spray

1. In a bowl, combine all the ingredients except the cooking spray and stir well. Grease a pie pan that fits the air fryer with the cooking spray, pour the mixture inside, put the pan in the air fryer and cook at 360 degrees F for 35 minutes.
2. Slice and serve warm.

Shortbread Fingers

Prep Time: 5 minutes | Cook Time: 20 minutes | Serves 10

- 1½ cups butter
- 1 cup flour
- ¾ cup sugar
- Cooking spray

1. Preheat your Air Fryer to 350°F.
2. In a bowl. combine the flour and sugar.
3. Cut each stick of butter into small chunks. Add the chunks into the flour and the sugar.
4. Blend the butter into the mixture to combine everything well.
5. Use your hands to knead the mixture, forming a smooth consistency.
6. Shape the mixture into 10 equal-sized finger shapes, marking them with the tines of a fork for decoration if desired.
7. Lightly spritz the Air Fryer basket with the cooking spray. Place the cookies inside, spacing them out well.
8. Bake the cookies for 12 minutes.
9. Let cool slightly before serving. Alternatively, you can store the cookies in an airtight container for up to 3 days.

Cream Cheese Scones

Prep Time: 20 minutes | Cook Time: 10 minutes | Serves 4

- 4 oz almond flour
- ½ teaspoon baking powder
- 1 teaspoon lemon juice
- ¼ teaspoon salt
- 2 teaspoons cream cheese
- ¼ cup coconut cream
- 1 teaspoon vanilla extract
- 1 tablespoon Erythritol
- 1 tablespoon heavy cream
- Cooking spray

1. In the mixing bowl mix up almond flour, baking powder, lemon juice, and salt. Add cream cheese and stir the mixture gently. Mix up vanilla extract and coconut cream in the separated bowl. Add the coconut cream mixture in the almond flour mixture. Stir it gently and then knead the dough. Roll up the dough and cut it on squares (scones).
2. Preheat the air fryer to 360F. Spray the air fryer basket with cooking spray and put the scones inside air fryer in one layer. Cook the scones for 10 minutes or until they are light brown. Then cool the scones to the room temperature.
3. Meanwhile, mix up heavy cream and Erythritol. Then brush every scone with a sweet cream mixture.

Almond Orange Cake

Prep Time: 3 minutes | Cook Time: 20 minutes | Serves 6

- 1/3 cup almonds, chopped
- 3 tablespoons orange marmalade
- 1 stick butter
- ½ teaspoon allspice, ground
- ½ teaspoon anise seed, ground
- ½ teaspoon baking powder
- 1 teaspoon baking soda
- 6-ounces almond flour
- 2 tablespoons Truvia for baking
- 2 eggs plus 1 egg yok, beaten
- Olive oil cooking spray for pans

1. Lightly grease cake pan with olive oil cooking spray. Mix the butter and Truvia until nice and smooth. Fold in the eggs, almonds, marmalade; beat again until well mixed.
2. Add flour, baking soda, baking powder, allspice, star anise and ground cinnamon. Bake in the preheated air-fryer at 310°Fahrenheit for 20-minutes.

Sugar Butter Fritters
Prep Time: 10 minutes | Cook Time: 30 minutes | Serves 16

- 4 cups flour
- 1 tsp. kosher salt
- 1 tsp. sugar
- 3 tbsp. butter, at room temperature
- 1 packet instant yeast
- 1 ¼ cups lukewarm water
- 1 cup sugar
- Pinch of cardamom
- 1 tsp. cinnamon powder
- 1 stick butter, melted

1. Place all of the ingredients in a large bowl and combine well.
2. Add in the lukewarm water and mix until a soft, elastic dough forms.
3. Place the dough on a lightly floured surface and lay a greased sheet of aluminum foil on top of the dough. Refrigerate for 5 to 10 minutes.
4. Remove it from the refrigerator and divide it in two. Mold each half into a log and slice it into 20 pieces.
5. In a shallow bowl, combine the sugar, cardamom and cinnamon.
6. Coat the slices with a light brushing of melted butter and the sugar.
7. Spritz Air Fryer basket with cooking spray.
8. Transfer the slices to the fryer and air fry at 360°F for roughly 10 minutes. Turn each slice once during the baking time.
9. Dust each slice with the sugar before serving.

Air-Fried Apricots in Whiskey Sauce
Prep Time: 5 minutes | Cook Time: 35 minutes | Serves 4

- 1 lb. apricot, pitted and halved
- ¼ cup whiskey
- 1 teaspoon pure vanilla extract
- ½ stick butter, room temperature
- ½ cup maple syrup sugar-free

1. In a small saucepan over medium heat, heat the maple syrup, vanilla, butter; simmer until the butter is melted. Add the whiskey and stir to combine. Arrange the apricots on the bottom of lightly greased baking dish.
2. Pour the sauce over the apricots; scatter whole cloves over the top. Then, transfer the baking dish to the Preheated air-fryer. Air-fry at 380°Fahrenheit for 35-minutes.

Date & Hazelnut Cookies
Prep Time: 5 minutes | Cook Time: 20 minutes | Serves 10

- 3 tablespoons sugar-free maple syrup
- 1/3 cup dated, dried
- ¼ cup hazelnuts, chopped
- 1 stick butter, room temperature
- ½ cup almond flour
- ½ cup corn flour
- 2 tablespoons Truvia for baking
- ½ teaspoon vanilla extract
- 1/3 teaspoon ground cinnamon
- ½ teaspoon cardamom

1. Firstly, cream the butter with Truvia and maple syrup until mixture is fluffy. Sift both types of flour into bowl with butter mixture. Add remaining ingredients. Now, knead the mixture to form a dough; place in the fridge for 20-minutes.
2. To finish, shape the chilled dough into bite-size balls; arrange them on a baking dish and flatten balls with back of spoon. Bake the cookies for 20-minutes at 310°Fahrenheit.

Berry Pie
Prep Time: 5 minutes | Cook Time: 20 minutes | Serves 8

- 5 egg whites
- 1/3 cup swerve
- 1 and ½ cups almond flour
- Zest of 1 lemon, grated
- 1 teaspoon baking powder
- 1 teaspoon vanilla extract
- 1/3 cup butter, melted
- 2 cups strawberries, sliced
- Cooking spray

1. In a bowl, whisk egg whites well. Add the rest of the ingredients except the cooking spray gradually and whisk everything. Grease a tart pan with the cooking spray, and pour the strawberries mix. Put the pan in the air fryer and cook at 370 degrees F for 20 minutes. Cool down, slice and serve.

Butter Donuts
Prep Time: 5 minutes | Cook Time: 15 minutes | Serves 4

- 8 ounces coconut flour
- 2 tablespoons stevia
- 1 egg, whisked
- 2 and ½ tablespoons butter, melted
- 4 ounces coconut milk
- 1 teaspoon baking powder

1. In a bowl, mix all the ingredients and whisk well. Shape donuts from this mix, place them in your air fryer's basket and cook at 370 degrees F for 15 minutes. Serve warm.

Appendix 1 Measurement Conversion Chart

Volume Equivalents (Dry)	
US STANDARD	**METRIC (APPROXIMATE)**
1/8 teaspoon	0.5 mL
1/4 teaspoon	1 mL
1/2 teaspoon	2 mL
3/4 teaspoon	4 mL
1 teaspoon	5 mL
1 tablespoon	15 mL
1/4 cup	59 mL
1/2 cup	118 mL
3/4 cup	177 mL
1 cup	235 mL
2 cups	475 mL
3 cups	700 mL
4 cups	1 L

Weight Equivalents	
US STANDARD	**METRIC (APPROXIMATE)**
1 ounce	28 g
2 ounces	57 g
5 ounces	142 g
10 ounces	284 g
15 ounces	425 g
16 ounces (1 pound)	455 g
1.5 pounds	680 g
2 pounds	907 g

Volume Equivalents (Liquid)		
US STANDARD	**US STANDARD (OUNCES)**	**METRIC (APPROXIMATE)**
2 tablespoons	1 fl.oz.	30 mL
1/4 cup	2 fl.oz.	60 mL
1/2 cup	4 fl.oz.	120 mL
1 cup	8 fl.oz.	240 mL
1 1/2 cup	12 fl.oz.	355 mL
2 cups or 1 pint	16 fl.oz.	475 mL
4 cups or 1 quart	32 fl.oz.	1 L
1 gallon	128 fl.oz.	4 L

Temperatures Equivalents	
FAHRENHEIT(F)	**CELSIUS(C) APPROXIMATE)**
225 °F	107 °C
250 °F	120 ° °C
275 °F	135 °C
300 °F	150 °C
325 °F	160 °C
350 °F	180 °C
375 °F	190 °C
400 °F	205 °C
425 °F	220 °C
450 °F	235 °C
475 °F	245 °C
500 °F	260 °C

Appendix 2 The Dirty Dozen and Clean Fifteen

The Environmental Working Group (EWG) is a nonprofit, nonpartisan organization dedicated to protecting human health and the environment Its mission is to empower people to live healthier lives in a healthier environment. This organization publishes an annual list of the twelve kinds of produce, in sequence, that have the highest amount of pesticide residue-the Dirty Dozen-as well as a list of the fifteen kinds of produce that have the least amount of pesticide residue-the Clean Fifteen.

THE DIRTY DOZEN	
The 2016 Dirty Dozen includes the following produce. These are considered among the year's most important produce to buy organic:	
Strawberries	Spinach
Apples	Tomatoes
Nectarines	Bell peppers
Peaches	Cherry tomatoes
Celery	Cucumbers
Grapes	Kale/collard greens
Cherries	Hot peppers
The Dirty Dozen list contains two additional items kale/collard greens and hot peppers-because they tend to contain trace levels of highly hazardous pesticides.	

THE CLEAN FIFTEEN	
The least critical to buy organically are the Clean Fifteen list. The following are on the 2016 list:	
Avocados	Papayas
Corn	Kiw
Pineapples	Eggplant
Cabbage	Honeydew
Sweet peas	Grapefruit
Onions	Cantaloupe
Asparagus	Cauliflower
Mangos	
Some of the sweet corn sold in the United States are made from genetically engineered (GE) seedstock. Buy organic varieties of these crops to avoid GE produce.	

Appendix 3 Index

A

all-purpose flour 50, 53
allspice 15
almond 5, 14
ancho chile 10
ancho chile powder 5
apple 9
apple cider vinegar 9
arugula 51
avocado 11

B

bacon 52
balsamic vinegar 7, 12, 52
basil 5, 8, 11, 13
beet 52
bell pepper 50, 51, 53
black beans 50, 51
broccoli 51, 52, 53
buns 52
butter 50

C

canola oil 50, 51, 52
carrot 52, 53
cauliflower 5, 52
cayenne 5, 52
cayenne pepper 52
Cheddar cheese 52
chicken 6
chili powder 50, 51
chipanle pepper 50
chives 5, 6, 52
cinnamon 15
coconut 6
Colby Jack cheese 51
coriander 52
corn 50, 51
corn kernels 50
cumin 5, 10, 15, 50, 51, 52

D

diced panatoes 50
Dijon mustard 7, 12, 13, 51
dry onion powder 52

E

egg 14, 50, 53
enchilada sauce 51

F

fennel seed 53
flour 50, 53
fresh chives 5, 6, 52
fresh cilantro 52
fresh cilantro leaves 52
fresh dill 5
fresh parsley 6, 52
fresh parsley leaves 52

G

garlic 5, 9, 10, 11, 13, 14, 50, 51, 52, 53
garlic powder 8, 9, 52, 53

H

half-and-half 50
hemp seeds 8
honey 9, 51

I

instant rice 51

K

kale 14
kale leaves 14
ketchup 53
kosher salt 5, 10, 15

L

lemon 5, 6, 14, 51, 53
lemon juice 6, 8, 11, 13, 14, 51
lime 9, 12
lime juice 9, 12
lime zest 9, 12

M

maple syrup 7, 12, 53
Marinara Sauce 5
micro greens 52
milk 5, 50
mixed berries 12
Mozzarella 50, 53
Mozzarella cheese 50, 53
mushroom 51, 52
mustard 51, 53
mustard powder 53

N

nutritional yeast 5

O

olive oil 5, 12, 13, 14, 50, 51, 52, 53
onion 5, 50, 51
onion powder 8
oregano 5, 8, 10, 50

P

panatoes 50, 52
paprika 5, 15, 52
Parmesan cheese 51, 53
parsley 6, 52
pesto 52
pink Himalayan salt 5, 7, 8, 11
pizza dough 50, 53
pizza sauce 50
plain coconut yogurt 6
plain Greek yogurt 5
porcini powder 53
potato 53

R

Ranch dressing 52
raw honey 9, 12, 13
red pepper flakes 5, 8, 14, 15, 51, 53
ricotta cheese 53

S

saffron 52
Serrano pepper 53
sugar 10
summer squash 51

T

tahini 5, 8, 9, 11
thyme 50
toasted almonds 14
tomato 5, 50, 52, 53
turmeric 15

U

unsalted butter 50
unsweetened almond milk 5

V

vegetable broth 50
vegetable stock 51

W

white wine 8, 11
wine vinegar 8, 10, 11

Y

yogurt 5, 6

Z

zucchini 50, 51, 52, 53

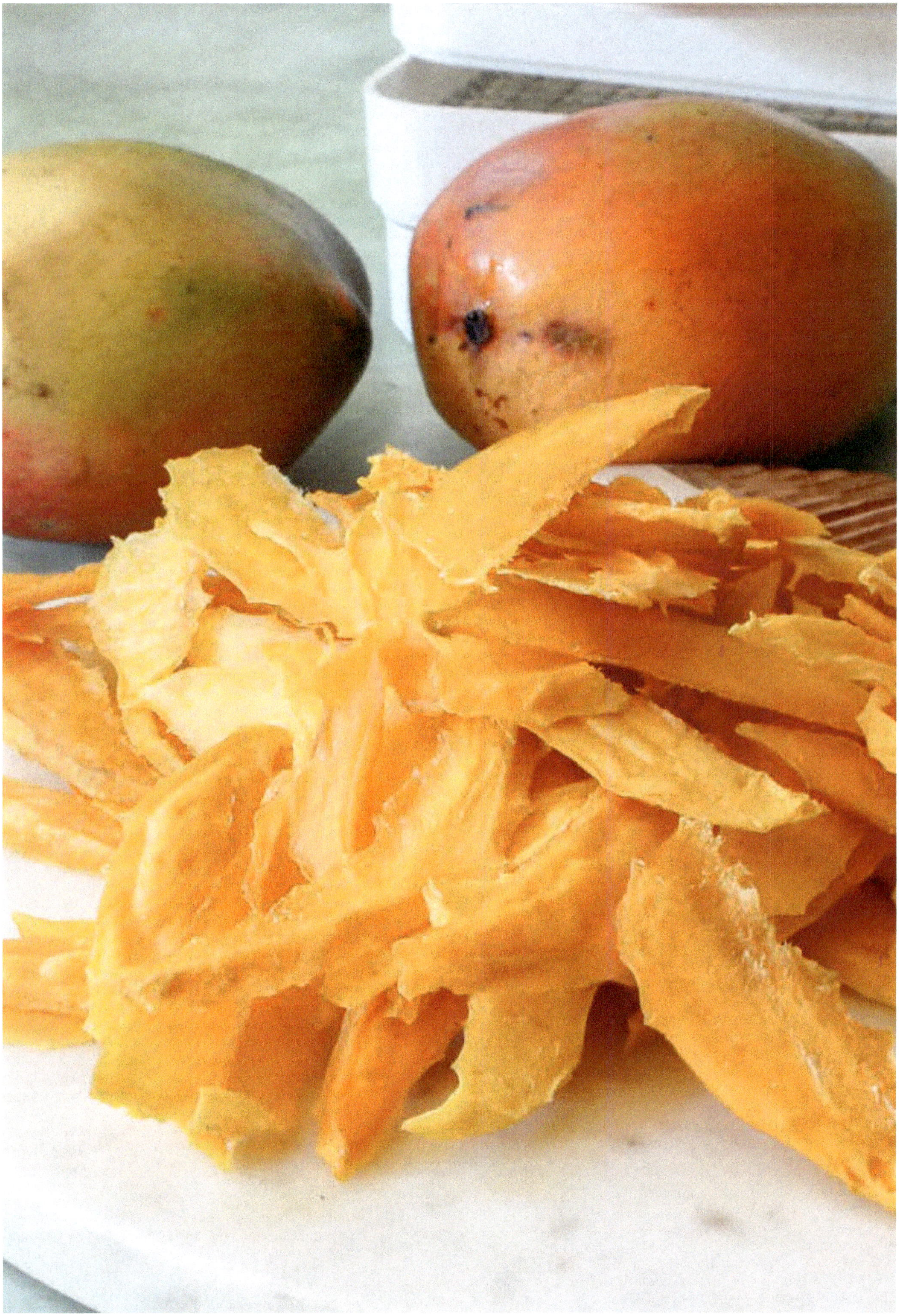

DORIS D. NORTON

Printed in Great Britain
by Amazon